ARCHITECTURAL DIGEST   CELEBRITY HOMES II

Celebrity Homes II

ARCHITECTURAL DIGEST® PRESENTS

THE PRIVATE WORLDS OF

THIRTY INTERNATIONAL PERSONALITIES

EDITED BY PAIGE RENSE

EDITOR-IN-CHIEF, ARCHITECTURAL DIGEST

THE KNAPP PRESS PUBLISHERS LOS ANGELES

THE VIKING PRESS DISTRIBUTORS NEW YORK

ARCHITECTURAL DIGEST® IS A REGISTERED TRADEMARK OF KNAPP COMMUNICATIONS CORPORATION

Published in the United States of America by
The Knapp Press
5900 Wilshire Boulevard, Los Angeles, California 90036
Copyright © 1981 by Knapp Communications Corporation
All rights reserved
First Edition

Distributed by The Viking Press
625 Madison Avenue, New York, New York 10022

Distributed simultaneously in Canada by Penguin Books Canada Limited

Library of Congress Cataloging in Publication Data
Main entry under title: Celebrity Homes II.
1. Interior decoration.   I. Rense, Paige.   II. Architectural digest.
NK1980.C42   1981   747.2'049   81–3786
ISBN 0–89535–048–3   AACR2

ISBN 0–89535–048–3
Printed and Bound in the United States of America

CONTENTS

FOREWORD

CELEBRITY HOMES II is a celebration of home. It is also a celebration of innovativeness and style, of color and creativity, and—yes, of glamour. In my travels about the world as editor-in-chief of *Architectural Digest,* I have noticed that, contrary to the often-expressed idea that the public likes to think of celebrities as being "just like you and me," most people enjoy seeing how the celebrity's way of life, as well as its setting, differs from their own. After all, if the celebrity's home—the actor's, the sculptor's, the statesman's, the couturier's—is just like everyone else's, where is the magic?

As with our first Knapp Press publication, CELEBRITY HOMES, and the succeeding books, AMERICAN INTERIORS and INTERNATIONAL INTERIORS, these residences have all appeared in *Architectural Digest.* Some are grand; some are traditional; a few are intriguingly eccentric. All are distinctive because they express the personal tastes of exceptionally creative people, who occasionally touch or startle us by the secret faces they reveal through their personal surroundings. Certainly none of these homes is cast in the common everyday mold. Why should it be? How could it be? The celebrity's *life* is not in the common everyday mold.

Yet there is a paradox here, of which every really perceptive interior designer is aware: The celebrity wants a home that is primarily a place in which to be comfortable. But comfort is a matter of interpretation: For Princess Margaret, it means an island home, on Mustique in the Caribbean, a home exquisite in its unstudied elegance; remote from the formality of Buckingham Palace and the exigencies of public duties.

For actor James Caan, it is a "country-style" residence in the midst of sophisticated Bel-Air; rich with Western Americana, with wide brick fireplaces and deep leather chairs; with Frederic Remington bronzes set off by the brilliant colors of Navaho rugs, on which the actor is an authority.

For couturière Zandra Rhodes, to whom "the house, like a garment, is a second skin," comfort is interpreted in a five-story London house with bare paint-splashed floors, scarlet walls and tented ceilings.

For French novelist and playwright Françoise Sagan, it means a Paris townhouse that offers "a wonderful solitude," and it is also a Normandy country house, spacious enough for a constant flow of guests when solitude has worn out its welcome.

Exciting, graceful, dramatic, these homes, presented in response to our readers' enthusiastic reception of the first CELEBRITY HOMES, unequivocally refute Sir James Barrie's wry observation that we cannot be both grand and comfortable.

Paige Rense
Editor-in-Chief
Los Angeles, California

ARCHITECTURAL DIGEST   CELEBRITY HOMES II

JOSEPH ALSOP

Behind a Federal façade in one of Georgetown's stately rows, Joseph Alsop—writer, scholar and host to statesmen—lives and works among his books and antiquities precisely as though he has always been here. In fact, he came to Georgetown forty years ago, just as this historic square mile was beginning to be restored and was achieving cachet among Washington's social and political luminaries. Yet Mr. Alsop, among the first to be captivated by the neighborhood's urbane dignity and charm, is a rather recent resident of the elegant townhouse, built in the early nineteenth century, he presently occupies. Even a hundred years ago the location was prime. Georgetown at that time was a flourishing port town, bordering the fledgling Federal City and, as Mr. Alsop says with what appears to be a good deal of pride, "only twenty minutes from the Capitol by horse."

The house seems entirely appropriate for a man who, besides having had a prominent career as a political journalist, has been a lifelong student of the past. A sense of history is everywhere evident in his house—from the gallery of family portraits tracing seven generations, in the dining room, to pictures of ancestral homes, in the dressing room, to memorabilia from his own career, in the study. These personal artifacts are intermingled with eighteenth-century furnishings and a number of antiquities dating back to the third century B.C. "The house suits me very well," says Mr. Alsop in his meticulous New England manner. "The proportions are marvelous. There's nothing artificial or strained about it. It's purely and simply a very fine Federal home."

When he moved in, three years ago, the residence was already well known as the hospitable home of John Walker, former director of the National Gallery of Art, and his wife, Lady Margaret Walker. They are "dear friends," from whom Mr. Alsop now rents the house on a life lease. As part of the agreement, he did considerable maintenance work and, of course, outfitted the interior to suit his own distinctive tastes and collections. His objective was simply "to achieve a pleasant place to live." The thoughtful arrangement, however, has evolved into much more

than that. It is a masculine and very personal reflection of the resident's far-reaching interests and background. His style combines intellectual sobriety with a certain idiosyncratic charm—at once formal and gracious, radiating an elegance that recaptures the spirit of an earlier age.

Seated in a wing chair in the high-ceilinged study, bathed in morning light, with tea served from an old family service as he concentrates on a large reference volume, Mr. Alsop seems at one with the era when the house was built. The study, as it was in the homes of gentlemen of learning of that period, is an important place. "I made the house my own, so to speak, by installing acres of floor-to-ceiling bookcases, since I have ten thousand volumes." These form a recurring design throughout the house, but they are hardly here for decoration. They are well-read volumes, catalogued for easy reference: history, cultures and nature grouped in the double living room; art and archaeology paneling the walls of the study; fiction stacked even around the doors of his bedroom. Mr. Alsop views his immense library pragmatically, emphasizing the importance of cataloguing. "When you have a great many books, you may as well have none, if they're not catalogued properly—since you can't find anything!"

Mr. Alsop is hardly a novice in the area of furnishings and fine arts, either. For thirty years he has been a collector of French eighteenth-century furniture and early Oriental lacquerware, developing in the process a connoisseur's judgment and a scholar's background. He once designed a house along modified Palladian proportions, which he built in Georgetown, to display his collections to advantage. Both the dwelling and much of his collection were later sold, when he retired. He moved to his current home soon after, to devote full time to his lifelong avocation: the study of art and art history.

Mr. Alsop need hardly be concerned that his distinctive home appears fixed in any particular time or fashion, however. The environment he has created seems to belong less to any particular century than to the endearing vision of one particular man of culture.

OPPOSITE AND ABOVE: *The Living Room of Joseph Alsop's Georgetown
home reflects a highly individual mix of objets d'art and period
furnishings, books and the accumulated memorabilia of a distinguished
career as a journalist. "I made the house my own by installing acres of
floor-to-ceiling bookcases," he explains, "since I have 10,000 volumes." In
an atmosphere of warmth and culture, comfortable slipcovered sofas coexist
with finely crafted objects, including Philadelphia library steps, circa 1820,
a Boulle desk and examples of Oriental lacquerware and porcelain.
Damask-draped windows flank framed segments made from a Chinese
scroll of the Hundred Deer. The dark sculptured head is by Chana Orloff.*
FOLLOWING PAGES: *A gallery of paintings in the felt-wrapped Dining
Room depicts several generations of the Alsop family. The American
sideboard, attributed to Lannuier, exhibits Empire candlesticks and
épergnes by Thomire; the Louis XVI harp is a family heirloom. A set of
Duncan Phyfe lyre-back chairs attends the boldly draped table.*

FRED ASTAIRE

"I don't think too much about my house," says Fred Astaire. "I just enjoy it." The house itself is in the untraveled part of Beverly Hills, where narrow streets are known only to the residents and most houses are obscured by towering trees. On the road below, a number half hidden in green shubbery is the only indication that somewhere at the top of the ribbonlike driveway is a house: cool, white and patrician, overlooking rose gardens and the city below. It is elegant and quite unpretentious.

"This house was built for myself and my daughter," says Mr. Astaire. "She was sixteen at the time, and I planned it so she would have her privacy, and I would have mine." He gestures toward the side of the residence. "Her wing is over there; mine is here. She's married now and living in Ireland with her husband." He takes a picture from a shelf, a photograph of a white house set in acres of serene and uninterrupted green countryside in County Cork.

There is a long pause as Fred Astaire looks about his home, trying to see it in an objective way. He smiles as he says, "The entrance hall reminds me of the Oval Office in the White House. And those doors over there. I don't know why I had them put in!" He pulls out a decorative lattice door that partially divides the library from the bar and nearly obscures the living room beyond. "I had some idea these doors would be good at parties, but I've never used them—even when I entertain, which I don't do very often." A feeling of tranquillity suffuses the library, and the room makes no demands, offering ease and enjoyment and pleasure close at hand. Between two windows is a table for backgammon, a game Fred Astaire has enjoyed all his life. A primary focus of attention, the pool table determined the great size of the room.

"I've liked pool since I was a child, although now I prefer three-cushion billiards. I'm a fair player, not good enough for the really top players. The only ones I can beat are those who are worse than I am." His whimsical humor is accompanied by only a faint turn of the mouth, not quite a smile. "The builders said that the table was too heavy for a standard floor; so the floor is reinforced and very thick. The morning after the last earthquake, friends called to see if I had lost anything. Not a piece had moved."

Crowded into a corner of the bookcase is a group of Emmy awards, a special Oscar, some Golden Globes, and the British Academy award—their gleam illuminating the recess. "Theatrical awards are certainly nice to receive," he says, "but I also like my racehorse awards, which I've been lucky to win with a small stable." Given prominence is the Hollywood Gold Cup won by Triplicate in 1946. There are also pictures of Fred Astaire with his winners at Santa Anita, Bay Meadows and Hollywood Park.

Yet, among the trophies and memorabilia is a stuffed toy baby kangaroo holding a handkerchief, a tear in its eye. "I have six grandchildren," Mr. Astaire explains. "I like to keep a few things so that the youngest will find something to fool around with. It keeps them from throwing the pool balls through the window."

Fred Astaire does not look much different today than when he danced many years ago with his sister Adele, who died in 1981. "Dellie and I," he says, "were very close. Both of us had so much to laugh about, and we visited each other quite often." He is a man so thoroughly in the present that one has the feeling his past stage and film successes are dim memories pushed to the periphery of his thoughts by his busy life in films today. The memorabilia that he does keep around seem to have a deeper kind of meaning for him. For example, there is a photograph of Ira and George Gershwin; another of a young and attractive man, signed "Cole"; and—in a small frame—a note, written in a beautiful hand, from the poet Jean Cocteau.

Mr. Astaire's bedroom serves his needs with a television, a desk and a small piano. It is here that he writes music. "When I have nothing else to do, then the music comes to me." He slides onto the piano bench and begins to play and sing his new, now familiar melody—the title song of Tony Bennett's album, *Life Is Beautiful*. The choice of song is surely random, yet in a curious way it is not. Life is beautiful, and that—for Fred Astaire—seems to say everything.

Fred Astaire lives the way he dances—with grace and style. ABOVE: The Living Room of his secluded residence in Beverly Hills is designed for tranquil comfort. The painting over the mantel is by Max Gunther; the larger canvas adorning the deep-toned wall is the work of Mr. Astaire's son-in-law, Richard McKenzie.
LEFT: The Living Room opens onto a slate terrace that faces the pool and a rose garden. "Deer come up and eat the buds," says Mr. Astaire.

In the Dining Room, cool-hued
walls and a simplified East Indian
rug offer a restful foil for a
dignified ensemble of period English
furnishings; cushions lend a note of
informality to the suite of Sheraton
chairs. Providing gleaming highlights
is a collection of Georgian silver.
The painting, which evokes a serene
classical dreamscape, is by another
member of this talented family, Mr.
Astaire's daughter, Ava.

FAR LEFT, ABOVE AND LEFT:
*Ennobling the Library is a portrait
of Triplicate, a winning racehorse
out of Mr. Astaire's stable in the
1940s. Awards in a bookcase include a special Oscar and several
Emmys and Golden Globes. Amusing bird paintings by Irving Berlin
are sentimental favorites. The tabletop holds personal photographs.*

GEOFFREY BEENE

Of all the professions in the late twentieth century, one of the most paradoxical and complex is that of the fashion designer. His clothes must be serious, that is to say, wearable, but at the same time they must bear the signature of luxury, even frivolity, in order to fulfill the fantasies of the purchaser, who is implicitly paying for the promise of a way of life behind the designer's label. And, indeed, many of the talented elite in American fashion do lead lives that are studded with public engagements, promoting at least the illusion of sophisticated and hectic worldliness. This is emphatically not true of Geoffrey Beene. He is a reticent, almost shy man, yet season after season his designs, thoughtful and never superficial interpretations of the style needs of Americans, are acknowledged by connoisseurs of fashion to be no less than superb.

As is so often the case with those whose lives are dedicated to the pursuit of an ideal, Geoffrey Beene is a subtle man who has a great deal to say about his approach to life—and to work. For him the two are inextricably linked.

He attended medical school, an unusual background for a fashion designer. "When you stop to think of it," he says, "it's really invaluable training. Learning how the body truly *works* has, I feel, given me extra sensitivity in designing clothes that move with, rather than against, a person." And certainly the crisp elegance of Mr. Beene's Manhattan apartment has as much to do with ergonomics—the study of the body in relation to design—as with the demands of style.

This is not to say that the designer's duplex apartment, for which Philip Haight provided architectural work, is less than highly luxurious. On the contrary, it is a contemporary epitome of luxury and provides an insight into how Mr. Beene orders his particular universe.

"Let me say that I'm very visual, obviously, and that I'm much taken with the idea of the interrelationship of all visual disciplines. The basic problems of color and proportion are there to be dealt with, whether you're designing a dressing room or a dress. But let's talk about the same givens that I discussed with Philip. Modern life— and I believe in being completely of my own

time—requires low maintenance. If you don't want a household staff, a space that is easy to clean and looks immaculate is a first priority.

"Then there's the question of materials, a vital one for me. I've always enjoyed mixing fabrics in my collections—tweed with chiffon, for example, or leather with metallic thread. Philip provided this for me in my environment by juxtaposing black lacquer with brushed stainless steel. I don't think a person should ever be overwhelmed by too much design. I wanted everything to be unobtrusive, so that people and flowers and sculpture would be very visible."

It was with sculpture in mind that Philip Haight began work on the double-storied space. To achieve this effect he opened all doorways to ceiling height and specified doors that slide into the walls wherever possible. The most important organizing element, an eight-foot-wide stainless-steel column, rises at the center of the apartment.

That the apartment should be a very private and rather exclusive world is not surprising; that Geoffrey Beene should collaborate with such a rigorous designer as Philip Haight is both surprising and encouraging. "I find it exhilarating to work with people whose talents I respect," says Mr. Beene. And Philip Haight explains the challenge: "We often wonder what it must be like to work with a person who has achieved fame in his own field. And, as far as I am concerned, it surely wasn't a disappointment. I did what I set out to accomplish. I wanted to make a backdrop appropriate to Geoffrey's way of living."

The architect has unquestionably succeeded, but clearly the catalytic nature of Geoffrey Beene's individual tastes and talent for the occasional visual bon mot is what endows his environment with its own sense of solidity and coherence. "I never look back," says Mr. Beene. "What's done is done." Cryptic though this remark may be, it nevertheless sums up his living space, a space that gives a concrete illustration of his approach to life, and to design. That approach is elegant and contemporary, and it is more than fitting that his New York apartment should give forth the satisfying air of existing thoroughly in the here and now.

To enhance fashion designer Geoffrey Beene's Manhattan duplex apartment, interior designer Philip Haight conceived a polished architectural shell that parallels the timeless integrity of Mr. Beene's creations.

OPPOSITE: *A suspended stairway with "swimming-pool" railings leads from the Entrance Area to the second floor. A wood and bronze torso by Michael Cohen complements Sven Lukin's wooden wall sculpture.*

ABOVE: *A massive shaft of stainless steel defines the Living and Dining Areas. A mirrored wall amplifies the space. Artworks include sculptor Ron Opferkuch's wire acrobat and a painting by Aizpiri.*

FOLLOWING PAGES: *On the upper floor, the same stainless-steel column serves as both the Master Bedroom's headboard wall and its main storage area. The twine sculpture is by George R. Bucher.*

CANDICE BERGEN

The time is early evening, a traditionally flattering hour, but Candice Bergen does not need any special effects to enhance her extraordinary good looks. She walks with a casual grace as refreshing off camera as it is on, and her humor and vitality are as appealing in a living room as they are under studio lights. Perhaps most remarkable of all, she has maintained this naturalness against the double odds of being first the daughter of a famous father, then successful in her own right.

Her gaze is direct: "Well, in a way this is my first grown-up apartment. I've lived on my own since I was nineteen, but this is the first time I've really put away my toys. No, I mean it! I had all sorts of souvenirs from childhood around me. Now that's all over, and I'm a serious person." Her smile suggests nothing of the kind.

Her apartment is in one of those eccentric old buildings that insisted on persevering through the perilous days of the great Manhattan building boom of the 1950s and 1960s. Now they are cherished as much for their indomitability as for their luxuriously high ceilings and marvelous views of Central Park. "I've always loved this building," says Miss Bergen, "so when I had the opportunity to buy an apartment here, I didn't hesitate. This is my East Coast headquarters."

Like so many older apartments that have passed through several owners, the duplex is in part a collage of history and taste. One owner left the two Art Déco bronze lamps that hang from the ceiling; another bequeathed the mirrored walls of the living room. "You see, this whole thing happened spontaneously. Much as I disliked the idea of possessions when I moved in—I was going through *that* phase—I had to concede that I need a sofa. And everything just seemed to develop naturally from there."

Soon she began to feel a growing attachment to the apartment. "Maybe it had something to do with being able to lie in bed in my little bedroom and just drink in the morning view. Or perhaps I got used to being expansive and generous about the park: 'Come up and see the spring view,' I'd cajole. 'Time for the snow scene,' I'd implore. Then, before I knew it, friends like Tessa Kennedy, Kitty Hawks and Ali MacGraw were picking vases for me, having chairs delivered. So I gave in and asked Renny Saltzman to help me put it all together—to make sure that all the armchairs were the same height, that kind of thing. I still don't know very much about interior design, and certainly I'm not an expert."

However, it is clear that in the process of furnishing the apartment, Miss Bergen learned to be selective. "Oh, my goodness, it used to be basket overkill in here. But I've eliminated a good deal. While I don't think it's ever going to be perfect, it *is* at a stage I'm happy with."

Certain elements in the apartment signal new directions in Miss Bergen's pattern of acquisitions. "I have mixed feelings about possessions. I mentioned my not-owning-anything period. Well, the opposite of that shows itself in such things as that willow rocker. It was made by Gypsies in the late nineteenth century. Then I acquired that tiny little chair in the same material: 'Son of Rocker.' Actually it's my party seat. It's small enough to be moved around, and I think it sort of endears me to people when I bring it out at a party."

She hopes that the apartment manages to suggest the seemingly contradictory qualities of the unpretentious and the unusual. But she feels that interior design is an ever-changing phenomenon. "I think I have a lot of refining and simplifying in my future. I haven't quite mastered the art of sweeping away, but I have always admired people who can live in a wonderful monastic space. I saw rooms in Japan that I found extraordinary; they were so calm and austere."

In the meantime, Candice Bergen is content to live in surroundings that combine elements of both exuberant decoration and sober refinement. While there is a sense that this compact duplex represents a work in progress, it is also a very durable environment—reflective of the generosity and vigor that she brings to all facets of a busy life. Just as her face has an incomparable bone structure—one that will outlive age and change—so does her living space reveal an underlying rhythm and coherence beyond the reach of any passing fad of style or design—or life.

"This apartment is all about familiarity," says actress Candice Bergen of her Manhattan duplex apartment in a circa-1915 building.

PRECEDING PAGES: *An unusual expanse of window upon window affords the two-story studiolike Living Room a superb view. With the help of interior designer Renny B. Saltzman, Miss Bergen established a clean monochromatic scheme, underscored by sisal matting and accented by the varied hues of books and pillows. A 1920s French poster of the dancer Mistinguett, at the balcony level, is reflected by a mirrored wall; the reclining nude sculpture, on the low rattan table, is the work of David Wynne.*

OPPOSITE: *Art Déco bronze lanterns punctuate the dark-toned and sky-lighted Living Room ceiling. Above the fireplace is a 19th-century Siamese temple hanging; an antique gypsy willow rocker rests nearby.*

ABOVE: *A mirrored panel interrupts the Living Room view, while a Tiffany poinsettia lamp translates the patterns of nature beyond. Over the elaborate African chest, an antique Buddha meditates serenely. Ledges at either side display family memorabilia and books about exotic places.*

ABOVE RIGHT: *A bold image by Jack Youngerman sparks the Dining Area. The lightly scaled setting—Mexican chairs, a glass-topped rattan table and a built-in serving console—continues the mode of functional simplicity. Bifold doors can separate this area from the living room.*

35

The balconied space above the dining area is Miss Bergen's Bedroom, where light-toned rattan furniture, small wall lamps and pristine bed linens harmonize with an ample antique mahogany partners' desk and a scroll-back chair. When bifold doors and window shutters are open, the area seems like a floating platform that reaches expansively toward the vista; when they are closed, it is transformed into a cozy room-within-a-room.

GOV. AND MRS. JOHN Y. BROWN, JR.

Cool country breezes float through the pillared portico of *Cave Hill Place*. "Ever since I was a child, growing up in Denton, Texas," says Phyllis George Brown, "I always dreamed of living in a house with huge white columns and lots of white plank fence. This is it—my *Tara*." The gracious antebellum mansion, hidden in the rolling hills of Kentucky's bluegrass country, a land of grazing Thoroughbreds, is the home of Governor and Mrs. John Y. Brown, Jr. It gives a welcome sense of permanence to two people who have traveled widely throughout their careers.

"No matter where we may live," says Mrs. Brown, "our roots are here. This is home to us." A former Miss America and award-winning television sportscaster, she combines charm and wit with a tireless spirit and drive. Her marriage several years ago to John Y. Brown, Jr., a vigorous and successful businessman—now the governor of Kentucky—has proved a matching of boundless energies. The couple's natural exuberance is central to the design of their home, a blending of unselfconscious elegance and comfort. It seems entirely appropriate for a hostess who combines glamour with warmth and a certain down-home directness: "We wanted a comfortable, country feeling, a place where people can come and be relaxed." Mrs. Brown refers to Cave Hill as a "retreat, a place to unwind" after her weekend commutes to New York City to fulfill her role as a television interviewer.

But it is quickly apparent that life at the mansion, both a private home and an official residence, is anything but retiring. On a typical afternoon the First Lady of Kentucky juggles several interviews, consults with the mansion's director and answers telephone calls—while bouncing her infant son, Lincoln, on her lap. Meanwhile, the governor receives visitors in his Empire-style study, an alternative to his office in the state capitol at Frankfort. Having held conferences in Cave Hill's dining room and conducted cabinet meetings at fireside, he confesses, "I hate to leave this place. It's so beautiful and peaceful here."

The mansion's inviting atmosphere can be traced directly to the energy and vision of Mrs. Brown herself and to the assistance of interior designer R. Wayne Jenkins, of Louisville. Their achievement is doubly dramatic when the circumstances are known: The house was completely renovated and furnished in six weeks.

The scenario started somewhat grimly. The Browns had been living at the Governor's Mansion in Frankfort for four months, when the building was unexpectedly condemned. At that point, Cave Hill, built by a nephew of Patrick Henry, was little more than a historical curiosity. After decades of neglect it was in a sorry state. Mrs. Brown recalls the period of renovation with pride: "Needless to say, we all love a challenge. We had no furniture at the time since we had been living in the Governor's Mansion, which was completely furnished. Before we were married, however, I had been collecting glassware, silver candlesticks, paintings, malachite. I had many accessories, but nothing to put them on. So we got into the car and scoured the countryside."

She and the designer traveled farther as well. Because of time restrictions, pieces located in New York showrooms were duplicated locally, including the mahogany dining table. Many antiques were acquired through an aggressive approach to auction buying. On one occasion, Mrs. Brown purchased a Hepplewhite sideboard by telephone on Derby Day and had it delivered in time for the celebration held that night.

The mansion itself, a gracefully flowing series of intimate and open spaces, seems almost created for entertaining. The Browns have obliged with parties held as often as three times a week. Benefits are given frequently for the First Lady's state programs; she heads an educational project that helps the Appalachian region of eastern Kentucky and a fund-raising effort to restore the Governor's Mansion. However, the couple's hospitality goes far beyond official obligations. "We love activity," says Mrs. Brown. "We love people." Indeed, their home is surely a place for people, a country environment that is also most urbane. So the Browns have gracefully enlisted Cave Hill in the revered southern tradition of hospitality, using the best of past and present, the best of public and private worlds.

Soon after John Y. Brown, Jr., was elected governor of Kentucky, he and
his wife, sportscaster Phyllis George, discovered Cave Hill Place, a
romantic antebellum mansion in Lexington. With the assistance of
R. Wayne Jenkins, the home, built in 1821 by a nephew of Patrick Henry,
was totally renovated and decorated in a matter of six short weeks.
Lofty pin oaks and maples provide shade for the neo-Federal-style
residence; its Georgian portico was a 1916 addition.

LEFT: *A fanlight-crowned front door opens into the Entrance Hall, where an Oriental rug cuts an exotic swath. Silk, embroidered with golden bees—a Napoleonic design— covers an antique settee and chairs; a wallpaper border of cupids and swags extends the Empire mood.*
BELOW: *At home, Governor Brown works in his Office, at a Chippendale partners' desk. An Empire daybed anchors the seating area. A harbor scene by Etienne adds ethereal beauty, while Jane Wooster Scott's lively composition, commissioned by Mrs. Brown, fancifully traces the governor's journey to the statehouse.*

RIGHT: *Palladian-style windows contribute dignity in the Living Room, where the cheerful hues of patterned draperies and upholstery were inspired by the Browns' favorite colors. The large oak cabinet shelters Mrs. Brown's collection of crystal animals and other objets d'art.*

ABOVE: *The intricately carved fireplace surround and chimneypiece in the Living Room are from a 16th-century English estate. On the sofa is a Kentucky quilt, reflecting Mrs. Brown's interest in indigenous crafts.*

LEFT: *Plaid draperies and upholstery fabric sound a bold note in the Study, echoed by wool-covered club chairs and a rag rug. Antique ducks, family photographs and an English print season the medley.*
BELOW: *In the stately Dining Room, Kentucky artist Bud Burwinkle painted the dogwood branches that bloom gracefully around the Venetian mirror.*
OPPOSITE: *Floral ebullience permeates the Master Bedroom, where an ornate Adam mirror overlooks a French country desk.*

JAMES CAAN

North of Bel-Air's lushly wooded canyons is where actor and Americana collector James Caan resides—"not near the mansionees," as he jokingly refers to the owners of grand estates that are nearer Sunset Boulevard, in Los Angeles. "I couldn't live in a fancy house where you feel funny lazing around, and you're always thinking, 'Oops, don't put your foot or hand there.' Actually, I'm the kind of person who never wants to go downstairs once I'm home. I live in my bedroom, which is of raw pine. I told Robert Cory, my interior designer, that I love Connecticut farmhouse smells. I guess the outdoors is what I want indoors, and that comes from cowboyin' as much as I do."

Since Mr. Caan collects Frederic Remington bronze sculptures and also Charles Russell paintings—his friends say he is almost happier being a cowboy than an actor—he points out that his house may seem, at first glance, to be entirely filled with western Americana. But there are also a French *bonnetière*, an antique captain's desk, signed Handel lamps that are as coveted as their Tiffany counterparts, and other vintage pieces that have nothing to do with the West.

"Today, many people tell me how valuable some of my art and furniture is, but I never buy anything to sell it. The Navaho and Yea rugs, which are dyed with natural vegetable colors and take months to make, have escalated in value, and frankly I don't know what they're worth today. I like them, period; that's why I live with them. One of my favorites is the ceremonial rug in the bedroom, with its figures of Indian braves, cornstalks, symbols of food, and always the one gray line that leads the evil spirits out of the house. If they're too tightly loomed, you won't see any holes, and that means they aren't good Navahos. When you hold a fine Navaho against the sunlight, some holes should come through, since the Indian women occasionally drop a stitch as they work. Another favorite of mine is the *Red Mesa*, with its incredible detail and wonderful combination of colors."

Mr. Caan's finely wrought Remington sculptures—*Cheyenne* and *Bronco Buster*—also express his enduring interest in the American West.

"Only a few hundred of these were struck," he says, adding that he bought them ten years ago for relatively little, and now they have appreciated a good deal. "Perhaps my most valuable painting, funnily enough, is of a clown's face, a portrait my dad gave me as a birthday present. The clown isn't very valuable in terms of money, but it means a good deal to me sentimentally, because it pleases my eye and makes me laugh. My father liked to collect, and maybe that's how I caught the collecting fever. He bought whatever caught his fancy."

The actor recalls that he asked designer Robert Cory, who restructured the upstairs—the bedroom and gym, complete with bath and spa—to include in the house six working fireplaces and "big floppy furniture—and wood, lots of wood."

Mr. Caan has nothing but praise for the interior designer: "Cory is the kind of man who doesn't talk too much, which I like, and I asked him to be creative. I didn't want to dictate to him. The entire concept of the house is his, and what he's done with the upstairs is what I've wanted all my life. There's also humor in what he's designed. My bathroom sink is an old dough-mixing bowl, long as a trough, and the shower is brick-walled, without a door—big enough for me to do acrobatics in, if I wanted. Everything is hidden behind the walls in my bedroom: television, stereo for my records and tapes, and a refrigerator for strawberry yogurt."

Initially built by actress Maureen O'Hara as a mountain lodge, the house has a definite country feeling. Coyotes and songbirds frequent the area, and James Caan can walk outdoors from his bedroom, along a rough-hewn walkway designed by Mr. Cory, to swim or sit with his son, Scott, near a rock, breathe the good air—and, as he says, "not know I'm in the big city."

In many ways, it is a dream come true. The actor loves his work, but cannot bear to be away from horses or cowboys too long. His house is an extension of his passion for the outdoors, and his philosophy, worked in needlepoint and framed, is near the front entrance: "May your horse never stumble, your cinch never break, your belly not grumble, your heart never ache."

Actor James Caan relishes the western emphasis designer Robert Cory created for the film star's Bel-Air country-style residence. Reflecting his prize-winning rodeo performances offscreen, Mr. Caan's film career is seasoned with Westerns. Art of the American West, collected by Mr. Caan, weaves a vigorous theme among the Living Room's woods, brick and deep-toned leather. Navaho rugs counterpoint dynamic bronzes by Frederic Remington and a Buck McCain painting over the hearth. Emphatic placement accentuates rug designs: **Red Mesa** *on the wall and* **Ganada Red** *between the sofas.*

OPPOSITE ABOVE: *A Remington bronze in the Living Room captures the tumultuous spirit of the Wild West. Peaceful accents—a Bradley & Hubbard lamp and a stained glass window—shine like jewels in the subdued setting.*
OPPOSITE BELOW: *Lacking only a horse, the Breakfast Area presents a distinctive western composition. Amid photographs celebrating Mr. Caan's rodeo adventures, the bronze sculpture in the corner depicts a cowboy; against the wall, a lariat is coiled in readiness.*
LEFT: *Echoing a bay of doors and windows, the circular Dining Room table rests on a subtle-hued durrie rug. A herringbone design enlivens the beam-framed brick fireplace.*

In the Master Bedroom Suite, which includes a gym with bath and spa, the designer devised a rough-hewn haven for Mr. Caan. The deft blend of architectural elements combines half-timbered walls and handcrafted wood floors.

LEFT: *Within the Master Bedroom's honed simplicity, bent-willow chairs made in the Ozarks, Navaho Yea rugs and a patchwork quilt bespeak the artistry of American craftsmanship. A Pairpoint lamp glows beneath a Gordon Phillips painting,* Tracks Snowed Under; *a Handel lamp is next to the bed.*

OPPOSITE ABOVE: *A brick shower and a dough-mixing trough used as a washbasin are imaginative additions to the airy Gym.*

OPPOSITE BELOW: *When the windows are open, luxuriating in the Spa resembles outdoor bathing.*

ALEXANDER CALDER

Tucked away among apple orchards and vineyards along the banks of the river Indre in the French region of La Touraine lies the small village of Saché. The river meanders past poplar trees, farms and an occasional château. At first sight it seems as if nothing has changed in this valley since it inspired Balzac to write his romantic tale *Le Lys dans la vallée* more than a hundred years ago. Until, near a house on top of a hill, an unexpected flurry of colors catches the eye. The bright red, blue and yellow mobiles of Alexander Calder are moving in the breeze, leaving no doubt that this is indeed very much the twentieth century.

Les Caldèrs—as the local people were accustomed to call the American artist, who died in 1976, and his wife, Louisa—made their home in Saché for the last two decades or so of Calder's life. Even before that, however, they were no strangers to France, having lived in Paris in the early 1930s. When they sailed back to Europe in the spring of 1953, they had originally planned to settle in Aix-en-Provence, but on a chance visit to the home of Jean Davidson, son of the sculptor Jo Davidson, changed their minds. He had just bought an old mill in Saché, and next door was a small house that just suited them.

It had, as Calder remembers in his autobiography, a "phantastic cellar-like room with a dirt floor and a wine press set in a cavity in the hillside. At the time one could barely see anything in there, all doors and windows being plugged with loose stones. I thought to myself: I will make mobiles with cobwebs and propel them with bats!"

The house was put back in shape, and Alexander and Louisa Calder lived and worked in *François Premier*, as the place was called—and still is—for no reason anyone remembers today. But lovely as it was, the "cavity in the hillside" also proved to be humid, and the Calders reluctantly decided to build a new house on the hill.

The way the new house was constructed is a typical Calderesque story. There was no architect. The artist himself made drawings on small slips of paper and, together with Jean Davidson and a French engineering friend, he supervised the Portuguese masons during the construction.

The enormous ground floor living room dominated everything and combined all the vital functions in one area. It served as living space, kitchen, dining room and working area. Louisa Calder turned it into a veritable kaleidoscope of colors: her blue, yellow, red and orange cooking utensils were hanging on the whitewashed wall; the kitchen stove was framed by African masks; a dozen bright woolen rugs, designed by Alexander and made by Louisa on the table in a corner of the room, covered the floor. Mobiles floated from the heavy wooden beams high above, and small stabiles stood everywhere—on the radiators, the refrigerator and even the television set. The sun streamed through the windows, and in the greenhouse, which forms an extension of the room, sparrows were in the habit of chattering among the jasmine and bougainvillea.

The design of the large open living space was not a new Calder idea. In Roxbury, Connecticut, where they had bought an old house after returning from Paris years before, Calder had turned a roomy old icehouse into a studio. The workshop at a little distance from the house in Saché was another example of one very large undivided room offering plenty of space.

Alexander Calder, even in his late seventies, put in a regular five hours of work every day. He was much liked, if not always understood, by his neighbors. Some point out the sculptures to visitors with obvious pride, but others shrug their shoulders and find the gigantic outdoor stabiles—which tend to have names like *Long Nose, Big Spider, Spiny Top* and *Curly Bottom, Thin Rob* and *The Anteater*—incomprehensible. On Sunday afternoons the village children used to come and play hide-and-seek or climb on the more easily accessible stabiles. They were wont to discuss the pieces among themselves, and a small girl was once heard to ask, while looking at a white mobile, "Is this the dress for the bride?" and a boy explained that "those disks are all butterflies." When Alexander Calder, builder of circuses and supreme juggler of form and color within space, heard such stories, he'd say, "All my greatest admirers are under six."

PRECEDING PAGES: *The unmistakable stabiles of Alexander Calder enliven the French countryside near the small village of Saché, in the region of La Touraine; beyond them is the large one-room studio he designed, which is detached from the main residence.*

LEFT AND BELOW: *Calder also designed this stone residence for himself and his wife, Louisa. Braced by buttresses, the rear wall of the house rises up forcefully for forty-five feet. The more traditional façade includes a greenhouse that is an extension of the residence.*

LEFT AND ABOVE: *The Kitchen Area of the large, open living space is a visual feast of color, shape and function, casually juxtaposing utilitarian, edible and decorative components. Brightly colored utensils, baskets of every shape and size, and primitive and ethnic objects share space with fresh vegetables and fruit. Calder-designed rugs cover the wood floor, while the paraphernalia of artistic production crowds work tables.*

OPPOSITE: *As he dined quietly at a rustic table in the Living Area, Calder was surrounded by examples of his own innovative spirit; behind him is the thriving greenhouse.*

GEORGE CUKOR

The house is in Beverly Hills on a twisting, narrow little street that looks more like a setting in Europe than one in southern California. In the early morning there is a feeling of cool languor. Mockingbirds are heard in the trees, a squirrel scampers across the road and the sun shines thinly through the branches of the trees. A wall thickly overgrown with ivy rises directly from the shady street. It is high and long, and the door in it, not instantly visible, seems dwarfed and not of the usual proportions. Inside, the world turns brilliant, as suddenly as a scene changes on the stage. Here is a garden radiant with sun and a house reminiscent of a villa on the Mediterranean. It is the residence of film director George Cukor.

"The best times of my life I remember having here, in my own house," says Mr. Cukor. "It's been an intimate part of my life, my work, my friends—a great many friends indeed. As a matter of fact, we used to work six days a week, and usually on Sundays. I don't know how I managed it all, but we had lunch here. There were regulars like Katharine Hepburn and Irene Selznick and Vivien Leigh, when she was in town. Through the years, particularly during World War II, everyone seemed to come here."

The director turns to look out at the garden, the flowering trees, the gentle splashing of the waterfall. "It never occurred to me that I could live in California. I was a New Yorker and came here with the talkies. Now I can't imagine living anywhere else. I'm not a sun worshipper, either. But here I live close to my work, in country surroundings. By Hollywood standards I've lived here a long time.

"Originally the house was a little one, but I rebuilt it in 1935. The garden was nothing, and it was redone by an extraordinary woman, Florence Yoch. The rooms are more or less as they were when William Haines decorated them."

When William Haines designed the house, George Cukor did not impose restrictions or make demands. "Mr. Haines may have asked me some questions, and I may have asked him some. Although he did the house, that is not to take away from my personal taste and knowledge.

The house suits me perfectly, and I know I belong here. That was Mr. Haines's skill."

A lively and discriminating taste informs the rooms. Everywhere there are mementos: a silver box with an endearing message, signed "Marilyn"; a Renoir on the table easel, a gift from Vivien Leigh; and familiar faces look from the walls: Greta Garbo, Tallulah Bankhead, Ethel Barrymore. The house holds many pleasant memories for George Cukor, including a drawing of Ethel Barrymore by John Singer Sargent.

"I've known people for such a long time," says Mr. Cukor. "You see how they go through life, and how they meet it all. I've had friends who've known tremendous success—dazzling success, success greater than most people will ever know. Yet these same people have also had to go through tremendous tragedies and terrible despair. It's how they've managed to get through that I think is extraordinary—how they've been able to come to terms with life."

The house, like its owner, is in praise of people and offers innumerable delights: the quiet of suede walls, the gleam of a metal fireplace, the eloquence of drama softly played. Shelves reaching nearly to the ceiling hold books inscribed to him by their authors: Aldous Huxley, Anita Loos, Christopher Isherwood, Edith Sitwell, Somerset Maugham and many others. A great admirer of humor, Mr. Cukor once presented a walnut to a friend, who said, "Oh, how beautiful! It's like a Fabergé piece." So she put it into her Fabergé collection, where it still remains.

"I think the element of fun," says Mr. Cukor, "is the most wonderful element in friendships, as well as in working relationships. I don't mean the mechanical laugh—rather, a humorous sense of fun, a sense of the absurd. It makes everything so much more enjoyable."

And indeed people, new friends as well as old ones, have done much to create the gracious aureole of Mr. Cukor's home. The house still is a place of many triumphs, serving a man who shares with generosity his perpetual pleasures: humor, grace and extraordinary sensibility. The house is, literally, George Cukor and his life.

LEFT: *A sun-dappled lawn and tall trees create a verdant setting for the Beverly Hills residence of film director George Cukor.*
BELOW LEFT: *Canvas-cushioned furniture appoints the pool area.*
OPPOSITE: *In the Drawing Room, elaborate cornice and ceiling detail and a grouping of antique furnishings lend an atmosphere of easy elegance. Chinese Chippendale giltwood pier mirrors enhance the beauty of Regency chinoiserie lacquered commodes; Régence fauteuils are covered in Aubusson tapestry.*

TOP: *A pair of Louis XVI bronze sconces in the Entrance Hall illuminates a suite of gleaming antique grotto furniture discovered in Wales.*
ABOVE AND RIGHT: *Views of the Oval Room reveal part of George Cukor's important art collection. The copper cornice and fireplace, and lustrous parquet flooring, deepen the mellow quality of the room. The painting near the windows is by Graham Sutherland; works on the fireplace wall (left to right) are by John Ferren, Georges Braque and Juan Gris.*

RIGHT: *An elaborate velvet drapery treatment, Neo-Classical architectural details and Venetian parcelgilt blackamoors combine to effect an appropriately theatrical Dining Room setting. A Victorian épergne stands in the center of the Sheraton pedestal table. "The regulars would sit at the end of the table," the director recalls of Hollywood's halcyon years, "and when there were new people, they sat close to me."*
BELOW RIGHT: *A John Piper watercolor, a painting by Kaminski, and a Vuillard lithograph enrich a spacious Guest Room.*
OPPOSITE: *A photo gallery of famous friends lines a Hallway.*

MR. AND MRS. KIRK DOUGLAS

On a residential street well traveled for a city like Beverly Hills, and behind a stand of towering bamboo, palms and native trees, lives an actor of stature, Kirk Douglas, and his wife, Anne. It is difficult to believe that a house so close to the street could seem so far from the city, or that its view, gardens and plants—arranged as if for a painting and graced with a modern bronze from Yugoslavia—could be anywhere but someplace in Europe.

But Anne Douglas, a native of France, has arranged the house and its surroundings with great consideration and care. In remodeling, she shifted the focus of the house from the driveway to the side gardens; indoors, azaleas bloom under a skylight canopied in white. Art has been chosen for its delight and personal meaning, and the mood of the house is a joyful one.

"I have friends who are interior designers," says Mrs. Douglas. "But they didn't really decorate the house. I planned the furniture layout and the colors, and they gave me advice. A professional knows about proportion and spacing. They can pull a room together, but I like to work out the details myself."

A black Labrador bounds into the room, followed by a King Charles spaniel, followed by Kirk Douglas. "My house is a very personal place to me," says the actor. "For one thing, I spend a lot of time here. I have a company, and everyone who works for me has an office—but I don't. I work here, and I probably spend more time at home than most men. So, in a way, I am more aware. I realize how comfortable this house is, how much I appreciate it, appreciate the way my wife has arranged everything. Even the wood gives me pleasure." He rubs his hand slowly and lovingly over the edge of a game table. "A home is a very emotional place for me." The sharp ring of the telephone interrupts, and Kirk Douglas is out of the room and back to work.

It is this deep sentiment and personal attachment to objects and art that give the living room its agreeable warmth. Mrs. Douglas looks at the room's paintings and for a moment seems to be far away in thought. "When we were first married and came to this country," she says, "Kirk lived in a small house on San Ysidro Drive. It was done in black and brown and was very attractive, but the walls were bare. He was giving a cocktail party to introduce me to his friends, and I happened to mention to a friend of mine that there were no paintings in his house. She said 'Never mind. I know a dealer, and he will lend you some.' So we went to his gallery, and I picked up a few paintings. Well, the next day I was ready to return them, but Kirk said they would be hard to part with. As a matter of fact, we still have them. And so our collecting began.

"You know, every time Chagall had a show he wrote to us to make sure that the painting of his we have would be available. It was the only one from his Mexican period that he had any record of. I was brought up around art—my father was a collector—and when you see art as a child you develop a good eye. Kirk's main interest now is in pre-Columbian and African art."

The rooms of the Douglas house are arranged with one space blending into the other, accommodating the flow of activity from swimming pool to tennis court. "We're all tennis players here," says Anne Douglas. "Every Saturday—this has been going on for over twenty years—a group comes here for tennis. We start around eleven and go on until about five. Then people help themselves from an informal buffet. For evening entertaining, Kirk and I both love small dinner parties, usually for twelve at the most. I use the large table, and in that way we are able to talk to everyone. When I have larger parties, I use the round table on the lanai as well. Often, of course, we have informal dinners and go to the screening room to see a film. But, you know, if we didn't have that particular room, I really wouldn't miss it. I do think it's nice to go to a movie theater once in a while!"

Kirk Douglas comes down the circular staircase, taking the steps two at a time. "I hope we're not going out tonight," he says. "Nothing pleases me more than to hear we're going to stay home for dinner." He looks at his wife, and she nods and smiles. It is clear enough that Anne and Kirk Douglas have the same priorities and that they care enormously about their home.

ABOVE: *The Mediterranean-style Beverly Hills residence of Mr. and Mrs. Kirk Douglas is enhanced by lush landscaping, a pool and a tennis court.* LEFT: *In the Living Room, an intimate alcove effect was created through the use of ceiling drapery and glass shelving that displays pre-Columbian figures. Thai tables mix with damask-upholstered French chairs and a contemporary sofa upholstered in a gay floral fabric. Velvet-covered poufs add flexible seating. The painting is by Yves Brayer.*

LEFT: *Works by Chagall, Miró and Agam hold aesthetic parley in the Sitting Room. The lamp was made from a Thai temple figure.*
BELOW LEFT: *A travertine Library wall provides a striated backdrop for art. Included are a vibrant painting by Lorjou, and a collection of African carvings on either side of the fireplace as well as on nearby bookshelves. A group of small pre-Columbian figures occupies the mantel. The painted vase in the foreground is by Picasso.*
OPPOSITE: *In the Dining Room, silver sea creatures frolic on the Chippendale table. Paintings by Buffet (left) and Chagall extend the aquatic theme.*

LEFT: *A glowing fire adds to the inviting atmosphere of the light and spacious Master Bedroom. A delicate Italian bedcovering complements flower-strewn fabric used for upholstery and draperies; the carpeting establishes underlying unity, its color echoed in the harmonious medley of fabrics. Dark woods and porcelain objets d'art inject varied accents. Artworks are restrained in hue: The charcoal drawing over the sofa is by Brice; the painting above the mantel, by Buffet.*
BELOW: *Stepping-stones inscribed by prominent guests over the years lead from the terrace, across the back lawn, to the screening room.*

ERTÉ

Fantastic images of theatrical splendor seem to dance before the eyes. Crystal chandeliers gleam, and there are enormous bouquets of ostrich plumes, luminous cascades of gold lamé and rich fur draperies held back by bronze figures of black slaves wearing little more than pearls. Here a bed shaped like some incredible pagoda, and there a sleigh in clouds of mother-of-pearl. Visions tumble one upon the other: sofas covered with a multitude of plump cushions, waiting for a Schéhérazade to tell the tales of Show Business; glistening mirrored walls; a whirling kaleidoscope of colors—and everywhere renowned figures from the pageantry of the stage: Turandot, the Queen of Night, Camille, Monsieur Beaucaire; Madame Du Barry at the side of Gaby Deslys; Josephine Baker and Zizi Jeanmaire; the famous Dolly Sisters and the Rocky Twins.

All the costumes and settings for these figures —whether real or imagined, legendary or mythical—were created by Erté in the most magnificent and fanciful manner imaginable.

For more than a dozen years now the sketches for these many costumes, sketches executed in gouache, have achieved an important vogue among art collectors. Indeed, they almost equal in value those watercolors created by Bakst, master designer of the Ballet Russe, the man whom Erté considers his inspiration and teacher.

In his Paris apartment, like some sorcerer from *The Tales of Hoffman*, Erté opens a wall covered with drawings, revealing other drawings on panels beneath, and then still others. It is all like some marvelous book with leaves of glass. On them in delicate colors are the extravagant backdrops of the Folies-Bergère; on other leaves, the hanging gardens of *Kismet*, the fountain of Mélisande, costumes that could be jewels, and jewels so extraordinary that they could be costumes for the stars of the fabled Ziegfeld Follies.

The work of Erté, who has always been admired by music hall performers and the producers of spectacular reviews, is enjoying a welcome revival of interest, perhaps thanks to the popularity of Art Déco. The Metropolitan Museum of Art in New York has devoted an exhibition to him, and galleries all around the world have shown his gouaches and lithographs.

Indeed, Roland Barthes, one of France's most distinguished philosophers, has written an entire study on Erté. Three books illustrated with his work have appeared, as well as a volume of his intriguing memoirs, *Things I Remember*.

It is a wonderful and amusing book, recording the story of a young man of noble Russian family who preferred to make fashion drawings rather than follow the expected career in the army or the diplomatic service. There was the success that came so early: the incredible covers for *Harper's Bazaar*, the revues designed for the Casino de Paris, his glamorous appearance at opera balls in the company of exquisite women.

It comes as something of a surprise that this enchanter, so adept at creating the most fantastic milieus, lives simply in a small and charming apartment that has hardly changed since he moved in, some forty years ago. At the time, the building was new, and was considered very modern. Large bay windows overlook the Bois de Boulogne. Ceilings are low, and rooms blend into each other through large openings.

The general color scheme is beige. Walls and ceilings are hung with Japanese straw mats, and the floor is covered with a rope carpet from the Balearic Islands, where Erté passes several months in the sun each year. For the most part, chairs are exceedingly simple, in the style of Charles X, and tables and chests are Victorian. The board on which Erté creates his imaginative designs is made of simple unfinished wood, and perfect order reigns over his desk.

Yet here and there throughout the apartment are unusual touches that indicate the presence of an extraordinary owner. In the entrance hall there is a wall aquarium that can also be seen from the study; and in the salon, up near the ceiling, beautiful doves preen behind a pane of glass. The sun pours in upon them, and they are quite as content in their own "aquarium" as the fish in theirs. Two handsome cats—one Persian, one Siamese—share the apartment with Erté. They are as elegant and precise as the milieu in which they live—a milieu where not a centimeter is wasted, where there is never any disorder.

The Paris apartment of fashion illustrator/scenic designer Erté is as
original and precise as his imaginative creations.
OPPOSITE: *Set and costume designs by Erté for* La Traviata *enliven a
Living Room arrangement. The 1830 Italian console holds an Empire clock
and candlesticks; beneath the table is an Erté sculpture in wood and iron.*
ABOVE: *A wall aquarium enhances bookcases in the woven-straw-upholstered
Study; the orderly design is consistent with the adjoining living room.*
FOLLOWING PAGES: *An Erté retrospective of theatrical designs is
mounted within a cupboard of movable panels in the Living Room.
Doves-under-glass bask in the light-filtered window recess.*

RIGHT: *A dense cluster of sculptural seashells dramatizes the other side of the aquarium.*
BELOW RIGHT: *Personal memorabilia graces a tabletop in the Bedroom. The whimsical avian sculpture is by Erté.*
OPPOSITE: *Erté designs on a raised panel of his desk in the Studio; large windows and a terrace overlook the Bois de Boulogne. He prefers to work at night, alone except for his two cats.*

MALCOLM S. FORBES

"Which one do you think we should buy," Malcolm S. Forbes asked his son Christopher, "the Brueghel or the *Château de Balleroy?*" Two hours earlier, father and son had arrived at the Caen-Carpiquet airport, where Myriam Benedic, the former Comtesse de la Cour de Balleroy, and her husband, Hubert, had greeted them. A rapid drive through the Norman countryside had brought them to the château built for her ancestor Jean de Choisy almost 350 years earlier.

The tour of the château had begun after an aperitif. Mr. Forbes and his son were standing in the *Salon d'Honneur* beneath the magnificent frescoes of the *Four Seasons,* attributed to Pierre Mignard, when the question above was posed. By this time, however, the question itself was already rhetorical. As lovely as the Brueghel was, and is—and in spite of the fact that it would not require rewiring, new heating and plumbing, major roof and masonry repairs and maintenance, refurnishing or redecorating—there was no contest between the Flemish allegorical landscape and the earliest surviving work of the legendary French architect François Mansart.

"I was bowled over by this lovely château," Malcolm Forbes recalls. "Beyond the house was an equally stirring setting: a park planted with an avenue of 200-year-old beech trees, and the main street of the village laid out to create a prospect. Clearly Balleroy was irresistible."

It quickly became the crown jewel of a collection already assembled by Mr. Forbes, both as bases of operation for *Forbes* magazine's international activities and for many other reasons. Earlier acquisitions included a 12,000-acre Montana cattle ranch and the 168,000-acre Trinchera ranch, in southern Colorado, which contains some of the loveliest peaks in the Sangre de Cristo Mountains and the best trout fishing in Colorado.

In addition, there is the *Palais Mendoub,* once the residence of the quasi-independent satrap of Tangier, as well as *Old Battersea House,* a seventeenth-century manor situated in London on the banks of the Thames. Zane Grey's former fishing camp on Tahiti and the 3,500-acre island of Laucala in the Fijis complete Malcolm Forbes's present collection of properties. The last is a Pacific paradise: jagged peaks covered in lush green vegetation; rolling hills planted with coconut palms; white sand beaches sloping down to blue lagoons.

"Each of these properties is unique," says Mr. Forbes, "either architecturally or geographically—or both. Yet, even in such a group, I feel that Balleroy stands out."

Certainly, in the ten years since acquiring the château, which was built between 1626 and 1636, he has managed to make it entirely his own. For example, restoration was halted for two years so that the stables, fronting on the Le Nôtre-designed parterres, could be transformed into a museum of ballooning.

"Man's first flight was achieved in France, in a balloon designed by the Montgolfier brothers in 1783," explains Malcolm Forbes. "It seemed natural to me, therefore, that the world's only museum devoted to ballooning should be in France, and the stables at Balleroy provided a perfect setting."

The opening of the *Musée des Ballons* in 1975 was celebrated with a great international balloon meet that has since become an annual event. Every year over 10,000 people come to the park to watch fireworks set to music, exhibitions of hang gliding, parachuting and Norman folk dancing—and, naturally, balloon ascensions.

When not serving as the ballooning center of northern France, Balleroy continues to undergo a gradual restoration and refurbishment. It is classified as a national monument by the Direction Générale des Beaux-Arts, and the French government has participated in a five-year program of structural repairs. A second five-year program is being undertaken.

Some of the first steps of the restoration were turned over to the Belgian-born architect and interior designer Robert Girofi. A resident of Tangier, he had successfully accomplished the entire redecoration and arrangement of the Palais Mendoub for Mr. Forbes. And so the work continues at Balleroy. Slowly but surely the château is being returned to its past splendor—complete with present comforts.

Publisher Malcolm S. Forbes, an
ardent enthusiast of ballooning,
established the world's only museum
of ballooning at Balleroy, his
French Louis XIII–style château in
Normandy. The earliest surviving
work of renowned architect François
Mansart, Balleroy was built between
1626 and 1636. A model of French
Classicism, its innovative structural
features include the façade's
symmetry and emphatic verticality,
and distinctive mansard roofs.

OPPOSITE: *Its coved ceiling frescoed with an allegorical composition attributed to Pierre Mignard, the* Salon d'Honneur *resonates with French Baroque grandeur. Faux-marbre walls are ornamented with carved floral swags. The regal portraits are by Mignard and his school.*
ABOVE: Parquet de Versailles *flooring and* Régence *boiserie present a medley of lustrous woods in the Main Dining Room.*

OPPOSITE: *Elaborate plasterwork festoons the* Petit Salon aux Aigles, *and 19th-century engravings adorn the paneled and mirrored walls. Subtle hues link a modern rug from Kashmir with tapestry-covered Louis XVI appointments.*
RIGHT: *Discovering a prized Second Empire chandelier in 1978, Mr. Forbes invited Robert Gerofi to restore the Music Room as a setting for it. The designer removed partitions that had divided the room into a bedrom suite and duplicated the bedroom's paneling and plasterwork for the expanded salon. The delicate tones of the Savonnerie rug inspired the color scheme. The portrait is from the School of Mignard.*
BELOW RIGHT: *In the Library, an English influence governs French Second Empire paneling and bookcases. Russian silver and onyx ornaments embellish the mantel and desk. Above the mantel is a painting by Comte Albert de Balleroy.*

93

LEFT: *An abundance of cotton fabric envelops a Guest Room. Portraits date from the 19th century.*
BELOW LEFT: *The capsule used by Mr. Forbes in his attempted Atlantic crossing introduces the Balloon Museum's Main Gallery.*
OPPOSITE: *Mr. Forbes is particularly enchanted with the approach to the residence. In an early example of urban planning, Mansart specified that the village of Balleroy be laid out to create an unbroken vista leading to and ennobling the château. The forecourt's boxwood parterres, installed in 1890, follow 17th-century designs by André Le Nôtre. To their right, a former stable now houses the Balloon Museum. The moat, no longer filled, surrounds the residence.*

HUBERT DE GIVENCHY

"If I had not devoted my life to being a couturier," says Hubert de Givenchy, "I'm quite certain I might have chosen a career either in architecture or in interior design." Nevertheless, he delights in recalling the beginnings of his career in fashion. He first worked for Jacques Fath, who sent him to museums to study the history of costume and to consider antique fabrics and trends.

In such a way he was soon able to appreciate the evolution of style, not only in fashion but in interior design—to see clearly that one is more often than not a reflection of the other. During the Directoire, for example, the simplicity of feminine clothes *à la grecque* conformed to the purified furniture of the era. During the nineteenth century, on the other hand, clothes designed by Worth used many of the same furbelows found on the richly styled and elaborately tufted furniture of the Second Empire. "Then, as now," M. de Givenchy explains, "everything in the field of design interested me—from architectural drawings to sketches of gowns to fabric designs."

There is little doubt that his own interest in style and taste and design began at an early age. His grandfather was a collector and a painter—at one time, in fact, a student of Corot—and later came to be the director of the tapestry workrooms at Beauvais. His own collections were gathered in a large country house where, his grandson recalls, to look through them "was a fabulous experience for appreciative children."

Hubert de Givenchy's own apartment in Paris occupies a handsome floor in one of those private houses built at the end of the last century on the edges of the Faubourg Saint-Germain. Between the two World Wars the building was heightened and expanded by an architect of intelligence who respected the decorative elements of the nineteenth century. He unified the floor-through apartments by creating a large bay *à l'italienne,* forming a vast hall that suggests nothing so much as the entrance to a private home—and not simply the hall of an anonymous apartment building.

"When I moved in," M. de Givenchy recalls, "it was a time when heavy mahogany furniture and elaborate silver were popular. But all I really wanted was a comfortable and charming apartment. So I began to think about what I should do, and I remembered a phrase of Jean Cocteau: 'To be in fashion is to be already passé.'" This paradox—and two important discoveries—showed Hubert de Givenchy the form his own apartment would take. One discovery was a Boulle armoire he had seen long before at an exhibition. It had been purchased by the painter José Maria Sert and at long last was acquired by the couturier: "There are certain things, I suppose, one is destined to have."

Along with the acquisition of the much-desired armoire, a subtle masterpiece of opulence and sobriety, was the impact upon him of an apartment belonging to some friends in Rome, members of the Agnelli family. "It was filled with marvelous things, but there was nothing in any way excessive. In fact, it was a perfect mixture of the sumptuous and the simple. More remarkable, perhaps, was the blend of many different materials and many different styles—from simple cotton to bronze-doré, from Régence to metal garden furniture to the most contemporary of paintings. So when I came back to Paris, I had unconsciously reached a decision. My Boulle armoire needed no elaborate damasks around it! Right away I called the interior designer Charles Sévigny for his help and advice."

Even though he owns many paintings and statues and other objects, M. de Givenchy and the designer were rigorously selective for the Paris apartment. The result is that Hubert de Givenchy has been able to send many of his possessions to a charming retreat he has acquired in the country. Here he is absorbed in the restoration of a Louis XIII house, with an ancient courtyard and lovely old walls of white stone. Perhaps, when visiting this pied-à-terre, Hubert de Givenchy thinks back to his grandfather's house in the country where his own career in design quite literally began—as a young boy delving into armoire after armoire to discover what wonderful fabrics and objects were inside. For him, that youthful enthusiasm and curiosity have never diminished.

Interior designer Charles Sévigny has arranged a subtle setting of stylish
quality for couturier Hubert de Givenchy's Paris apartment.
OPPOSITE, ABOVE AND FOLLOWING PAGES: A Boulle armoire, with copper,
shell and bronze-doré decoration, is backdropped by a bronze-mirrored
screen that contributes reflective depth to the Salon. The desk is also by
Boulle. Displayed inside the armoire is a collection of "mirror-black"
Chinese vases with gold-toned motifs. The large low table displays a
17th-century Italian bronze horse and other black-lacquered vases on
bronze-doré mounts. The painting above the chaise longue is by Rothko;
above the sofa is a Miró. A slender Giacometti bronze figure
stands to the right of the elaborate armoire.

Dark, warm and intimate, the Dining Room is lined with bronze-mirrored panels that reflect the blaze from an oversize Louis XV fireplace (relocated from the salon). Lighting is low and diffuse, rather than concentrated at chandelier height. Collages by Braque, at right, and Nicolas de Staël, at left, are mounted on the mirrored panels, some of which conceal closets. Giltwood chairs, covered in warm-toned leather, are by Jacob. The mask is by Robert Courtright.

LEFT: *In a Bedroom, an opulent marquetry commode, surmounted by a bronze-doré* chaufferette, *contrasts with the spare geometry of contemporary furnishings and modern art. Paintings, from left to right, are by Kurt Schwitters, Ben Nicholson and Joan Miró. Lacquered panels at right are closet doors; those at left conceal windows.*
ABOVE: *Givenchy commissioned Arnaldo Pomodoro to execute a sculpture for the small Terrace. Its polished surface, slashed by a fissure, reflects the changing light.*

ROBERT GRAVES

"Gertrude Stein was the first person who recommended Majorca to me," Robert Graves likes to recall. "She suggested that if I liked paradise, Majorca was paradise." Miss Stein obviously preferred less utopian places, but Robert Graves was instantly attracted by the history of the rugged, unspoiled island. Phoenician and Carthaginian traders originally settled this and the other Balearic Islands, off the east coast of Spain, about three thousand years ago, and they were succeeded by the Romans. Such roots appealed immensely to the poet's classical spirit when he left England in 1929.

The air is heavy with the scent of ripe figs and anise on the approach to the writer's house at the edge of Deyá, a village that has long attracted artists. Deyá, Robert Graves explains jokingly, "is a corruption of *el pueblo de ya pintado,* 'the village of what has already been painted,' because every artist pitched his camp stool in exactly the same spot."

His home is on a rise just off the main road leading out of the village; it is a simple three-story limestone building with green shutters identical to those of the other houses in the village. Here, surrounded by the deep-green orange trees he himself planted in the early 1930s and a bit of manicured English lawn—so rare on these islands—the octogenarian poet lives with his second wife, Beryl, whom he married in 1939. He calls his house *Cannelun,* a word that more or less means "the house further on." High above the hillside on which he built the house "tower the sheer precipices streaked with rusty ochre and above those the bald limestone brow of Mt. Teix," as he has written.

With the money he earned from his early autobiography, *Good-bye to All That,* Mr. Graves moved Majorca with the American poet, Laura Riding. "After a few months at Deyá," he says, "I fetched my books and furniture from England. I was assured, correctly, that I should be able to live in Majorca on a quarter of the income needed in England. I chose Deyá, a small fishing and olive-producing village on the mountainous northwest coast of the island, where I found everything I wanted as a background for my work as a writer: sun, sea, mountains, spring water, shady trees, no politics, and a few civilized luxuries such as electric light. I wanted to go where town was still town; and country, country. There were other desiderata, naturally, such as good wine."

Although Robert Graves was attracted to old houses, he decided to build a new one "on the best site for miles." He and Riding drew up plans with a local builder/architect for everything from the wrought-iron gates to the warm, mellow tiles of the floors. Today the whitewashed walls of the five unpretentious rooms on the ground floor project a welcoming simplicity. The hall is graced by a set of early prints of Majorcan life. The main dining room, the adjoining sitting room and the library leading to the writer's study all have dark pine beams contrasting with the pale tiles of the floor.

Now that he no longer runs up the stairs three at a time, Mr. Graves sleeps in the library, amidst his favorite and most precious books. Cannelun was designed as a work place, however, and for nearly four decades the poet/novelist spent many hours a day writing in his study. The steel-nibbed pens still stand next to the inkwell on his mulberry-wood writing table, and the study is crammed with curious mementos: shells, magnifying glasses, Ashanti weights, bottles filled with colored marbles.

There are also some more serious items of décor: batik, an ivory-inlaid Chinese traveling chest of the eighteenth century in which he keeps various records, and a drawing by Joan Miró with a lengthy dedication to Graves. And then, covering the walls, are the books, including over 140 volumes of his own writings, from *I, Claudius* to numerous anthologies of his poems.

Cannelun has been Robert Graves's home since 1931, except for the decade between the start of the Spanish Civil War in 1936 and the end of World War II, when he lived in England. Here and there are many touches of nostalgia for the United Kingdom, however. Clearly the poet, though known to the Mediterranean villagers simply as "Don Robert," remains a transplanted Anglo-Saxon romantic.

Lured by the climate and classical heritage of Majorca, poet Robert Graves left England in 1929 to settle in the rugged hills above Deyá; here, favored by the muse, he has created the major portion of his oeuvre.
BELOW: *The residence, Canelluñ, which Graves helped design, was constructed "on the best site for miles"—a slope silvered by olive trees.*
OPPOSITE: *In the Master Bedroom, idyllic images of the landscape in northern Russia are by V. Kovenatsky.*
OPPOSITE BELOW: *Writing at the table in his Study, Graves tirelessly plumbed his major theme: "The practical impossibility, transcended only by a belief in miracle, of absolute love continuing between man and woman." Bookshelves contain copies of his collected poems,* I, Claudius *and many of his other works. The batik wall hanging is by Len Lye.*

RIGHT: *A Terrace affords an inviting spot for family breakfasts and for taking tea with guests.*
ABOVE: *As deft with a cooking spoon as with a pen, Graves invented his own recipe for the orange marmalade that brightens the Kitchen table. Wholesome comestibles complement his wife Beryl's collection of colorful Majorcan pottery and baskets.*

ABOVE: *The Living Room, graced by a sturdy Spanish cupboard, reflects the warm, simple life enjoyed by Graves and his family.* LEFT: *Adorning a corner shelf in the Living Room, a stone jar from Minorca represents a craft established when ancient Romans inhabited the island. Whitewashed walls set off a Baxter print of a boy and a depiction of a Japanese motif.*

GEORGE HAMILTON

George Hamilton had been looking for another house. Although the actor had homes in Los Angeles and in Aspen, he did not have the feeling of living with any real roots. "I was reared in the South and went to school in the East," he says, "and I wanted a combination of the two places." A seemingly impossible request, but then he saw *The Cedars,* a plantation in Church Hill, Mississippi, an old Tory settlement that still retained its eastern flavor. "I realized it was exactly what I had been looking for. There were no neighbors—only land as far as I could see."

Mr. Hamilton set about restoring the 160-year-old house, considered somewhat unusual in the National Register of Historic Houses because it illustrates the changeover from a planter's shack to a plantation house. He explains that the house was built originally with four equal rooms, two on either side of a central passageway.

When the first owner brought his bride-to-be to survey her future domain, however, she said, "I cannot marry you unless you give me a house with more style." Four rooms were added, including a ballroom, and the porch of the original structure became the link to this new addition.

Until the house was purchased by George Hamilton, little had been done to it. "The Civil War left the area here impoverished," explains Mr. Hamilton, "and a series of owners had not been able to do anything except preserve the house. I wanted to restore it properly, and advice came from all over. The best advice on the period, oddly enough, came from Hollywood set designers. My brother, who is an interior designer, and a young man in the area, Terry Scott, both helped, and Elizabeth Treadwell researched much of the restoration. Most important were the workmen, who were knowledgeable about materials, timber and such. Certain woods like blue poplar, cypress and cedar were used because they're resistant to the heavy humidity, which is ferocious, like a jungle.

"I wanted to modernize the house as much as possible. It doesn't make any sense to restore a house and have the kitchen in a cookhouse some place." Air conditioning was added, and contemporary bathrooms were styled in the turn-of-the-century manner. "Everybody loves a modern bath, but it's obtrusive in a house like this. The kitchen is appropriate to the house, too. My son and I might have breakfast in it, but that's all."

Restoration has become a popular undertaking in the South, and any time a plantation house is dismantled, there is a rush to acquire old bricks and shutters, doors and mantels. "If you can't find those things, you have to have them made," says Mr. Hamilton. "Restoration doesn't come in standard sizes. For instance, the bricks were made and stamped right here on the plantation. The width has changed on floorboards, so mixing them does not look right."

Mr. Hamilton had some furniture in storage, and other pieces were found in New Orleans. "We're not going about this house much differently than they did in the eighteenth century. We've mixed many different periods of French furniture, just as they did then. We've had to go to New York for fabric, which they also did then. Also, I've learned something about southern décor that is *very* lavish. It's called 'swag, festoon and garland,' and it means hundreds of yards of fabric for everything you do. Now I can understand how Scarlett O'Hara made a dress, a cape and a hat from one set of draperies!

"I've done what I wanted to do in this house, rather than duplicating the way the rooms were done originally. That would be pretentious. The verandas run the width of the house, and everyone loves to sit outside. In fact, several days ago I was sitting outside thinking that the house was all finished—when a sudden splash of honey came down, and I realized the bees had bored into the rafters again. But that's part of living in the South, and so is looking out between the columns and seeing moss on all the trees.

"My son loves it here. He has a matching pony to my horse and rides everywhere with me. He fishes and checks the animals and gathers the eggs. It's so good for a child to have all that. I love being here for that, too, and I hope I can give him a sense of heritage." And George Hamilton, in preserving the gracious spirit of the Old South, has done just that, while making a sensitive contribution to the present.

Southern amenity permeates The Cedars, actor George Hamilton's
Mississippi plantation residence, restored with the assistance of T. Mikal
Scott and the actor's brother, interior designer Bill Hamilton. The original
house, a planter's residence constructed circa 1820, was later enlarged and
architecturally ennobled in the Greek Revival style.

The Main Drawing Room reveals Mr. Hamilton's desire to refurbish
the mansion, he says, "in the style it's accustomed to." Soft colors
harmonize with the muted tones of the home's original tapestry-upholstered
and moiré-clad furniture. Gold-leafed window cornices were fitted with
draperies fashioned in the style of plantation days.

OPPOSITE: *An antique American table, circa 1830, and a crystal chandelier are the focus of a traditional arrangement in the Dining Room. French embellishments include bronze-doré épergnes, Sèvres candelabra and an Empire clock. The portrait depicts the Empress Eugénie.*
ABOVE: *French and German dolls adorn a steamboat captain's brass bed in a Bedroom upholstered in toile with a Huckleberry Finn river motif.*

OPPOSITE ABOVE: *A profusion of printed cotton transforms the Master Bedroom into an opulent retreat. Dark wood accents lend contrast.*

OPPOSITE: *A 19th-century mood pervades a smaller Drawing Room, part of the humble original residence that grew into the plantation house. American portraits solemnly bracket a large European painting. The photograph at left is of the actor's mother. Shimmering satin covers both the sofa and the small round tables that flank it.*

ABOVE: *The Veranda reflects the serenity of the pastoral setting.*

ROY LICHTENSTEIN

From the outside, it looks rather like a garage: plain wood siding, with a few windows here and there, and large double doors. Inside, however, a world of fantasy and Surrealism explodes—on the walls, the worktables and the floors.

This is the studio of Roy Lichtenstein in Southampton, Long Island, situated a few hundred yards from the converted coach house in which he lives. The neat neo-Georgian residence and studio sit in a manicured landscape about half a mile from the beach, and the quiet grandeur of the area is only one of the anomalies that surround the well-known American Pop artist. Roy Lichtenstein's work depends on the ironic juxtapositions of stark simplicity and farouche fantasy, of puritan practicality at the service of comic-book dream worlds. So it is a surprise to find the artist working in such a conventional setting.

His inventiveness has progressed far beyond those first "quotations" of comic cartoons blown up to grandiose proportions, work that enraged and amazed the art establishment of the early 1960s. At that time his approach seemed a deliberate insult to the Abstract Expressionist movement—to offer as "fine" or serious art these comic-strip images in which the formalized clichés of strip cartoons were transformed by paint and canvas into objects for gallery walls.

To be sure, since those days, his work has taken many different turns. Recently, for example, he has chosen to deal directly with overt allusions to Surrealist art. The fact is not surprising since his original cartoon-strip images were often based on a simplistic form of Surrealism. Using the visual shorthand that developed out of the necessities of mechanical reproduction, he has concentrated on such imagery to the point where it has become a personal signature. In one painting hanging in his studio, *Two Figures,* the viewer might well *think* there is a Max Ernst model, a Miró shape, a Picasso Cubist object, even a Tanguy outline—yet no known work is brought to mind. Roy Lichtenstein's art is a referential puzzle that brings forth tantalizing questions: "Is it? Isn't it?"

Recently he has been creating works that, for want of a better description, will have to be called sculptures. Although not in the round, and not in relief, these cutout images occupy real space. Again there are the familiar objects from the art classroom, the still-life props in his recent painting: the model stand with a glass of water, the glass itself enlarged to monumental proportions; a mirror; a floor lamp, with its rays shining down; a tea cup with steaming liquid. The rendition of these objects is simplistic and cartoon-like, but they do stand out, controversial and questioning fixed ideas. They are formalized in such a way that they describe not only the objects themselves, but also a feeling that is near-abstract and difficult to define. Their gigantism brings to mind the world of Gulliver, at the least of Magritte, where oversize objects are found resting comfortably in real space.

Once Couture admonished his pupil Renoir to stop amusing himself and get down to serious painting. "Sir," Renoir replied, "if it did not amuse me, I would not do it." And so Roy Lichtenstein says with frankness, "The work I do always amuses me, but it is not a joke. I think there is something funny about each of the figures I do. Not hilarious or slapstick, but funny in the sense of being odd, peculiar, off a little bit in some strange way." He insists that references to commercial objects in his work are simply holdovers from the past and have little to do with his present viewpoint. At this stage of his development he has moved so far beyond his original source material that he has succeeded in creating classics of their own kind.

Outside his studio, in the cool sea air, it is tempting to wonder why Roy Lichtenstein, whose name and style are synonymous with urban imagery, ever decided to move from New York City to Southampton. He explains: "My wife and I came here some ten years ago and rented a house for the summer. At the time we were going back and forth to the city, and it was all terribly disruptive. Then, a few years later, we came here one summer—and never went back. I felt that I could get away from a lot of city activity that was interfering with my work. But I miss the city now. We may go back, for the city itself is always vital and interesting."

ABOVE: *The crisply painted barnlike exterior of Roy Lichtenstein's Long Island studio gives little clue to the fantasy within; his converted coach-house residence stands nearby. The noted New York Pop artist decided to move to Southampton in the early 1970s in order to avoid the interruptions of city life.*

LEFT: *Inside the Studio, the primary colors of Lichtenstein's work emerge forcefully. The monumental entirety of* Figures in Landscape *stretches across one wall, while the* Cup and Saucer II *sculpture, at center, appears to be two-dimensional but actually occupies real space.*

ABOVE: *This tearful detail from Lichtenstein's 1977* Landscape with Figures *focuses on a greatly enlarged comic-strip image. The heavy outlining and Ben Day dots, which recall mechanical reproductive techniques, are characteristic of the artist's work.*

OPPOSITE: *Clear light pours into the Studio, whose spaciousness easily accommodates the artist's large images. The most recent of these striking canvases contain overt Surrealist references.*

RIGHT: *The essence of a water glass is captured by this painted-bronze sculpture. Placing the work outside adds another Surrealist aspect.*
BELOW RIGHT: *A close view of the cup and saucer sculpture reveals the superimposed layering of its painted-bronze cutout shapes.*
OPPOSITE: *Roy Lichtenstein creates a playful image, interacting with his sculpted bronze* Glass II. *Nearby sculptures include* Mirror I, Glass I *and* Goldfish Bowl. *Says the artist: "The objects are transparent or reflective, and the game is to translate them into a three-dimensional cutout." The painting to the right is* Landscape with Figures.

ALI MACGRAW

The entrance is deceptive. A worn latchstring opens a courtyard door that is part of a nondescript façade, and suddenly there is a jungle of flowers and greenery leading to the softly rolling surf. Pink petunias and fuchsias, pearl-white begonias, vermilion impatiens, gold hibiscus and giant ferns crowd the pathway to the white sand lying along the coast of Malibu, where actress Ali MacGraw has taken a house. "Everything in the garden is in pots," says Miss MacGraw, "so I can take them with me if I leave —190 in all!" There are cabbage roses in tubs, profusions of daisies in barrels on the patio.

"This is the only way I can deal with living in Los Angeles. I'm here with the clean salt air and with the endless acres of privacy that the ocean gives me. I look out at the sea, and it goes on forever. I never feel trapped." This is the perfect setting for a child, she adds, namely her young son, Joshua, whose father is the actress's former husband, film producer Robert Evans.

Caboose, a black Scottish terrier, and Adam, a golden retriever, scoot about, as do the family cats. Ali MacGraw is committed to living far away from Beverly Hills and Hollywood. "The residents here are not all in show business. There are doctors, real estate brokers, rock stars and writers, dietitians, all kinds of people—and it's healthier for Josh to go to the public school with children of parents like these who share my fanatic demand for privacy. I hardly see any of my neighbors. Nobody drops in without calling, and I certainly wouldn't think of popping in unannounced on anybody at all."

Miss MacGraw continues, "I spend more money on greenery and flowers than anything else in my life. I came here with my books, clothes and the Indian rugs I collect. I never again want to be tied down with too many possessions. Designer Sally Sirkin Lewis helped me choose the sisal rug in the living room, and we designed the sofa and the bed.

"This isn't a showplace—as you can see from the cottage-cheese-like ceiling and the pink-tiled bathroom! But the location suits me, the easiness of the upkeep, and the fact that I can pick up quickly and go elsewhere if I have to. I keep an apartment in New York, where I go every month. It's become an addiction. I leave for a week, go the theater, ballet, listen to jazz, see friends, walk, stay up late—and then return to the quieter rhythm here at the beach, where I really don't go out very much."

Her way of life, she concludes, is nomadic. "I want to be able to pick up and—shazam!—go wherever I want to. I can take my pillows, rugs, books, and move anywhere easily. But I'll take my 190 pots if I'm anywhere in the area."

Miss MacGraw likes personal touches—photographs of friends and family, mementos and favorite old magazines—strewn about. Padding around in her bare feet, she laughs about disguising the front of the yellow-hued refrigerator with photographs of Josh and his Little League friends, New England scenes—she studied at Wellesley—old postcards of movie stars' houses, her love letters to Josh, and a delightful hand-scrawled note from Josh to her: "I promise to do my homework and feed my cats and take my dog for a walk and not bother people."

His mother elaborates: "What I want at this time in my life is a place where an active young boy can feel free to play with his friends and animals or eat an ice cream cone without my getting uppity about his making a mess in the living room. The natural pine dining table and chairs are easy to look after, and I entertain simply, with peasant soups, homemade breads, greens from the small garden I've planted. Everything I have now is more or less replaceable. I've moved so many times I'm released from the drive to live with mother-of-pearl chests and French sofas!"

On her stereo, soft contemporary music alternates with Mozart sonatas. She is certain that anyone can make life exciting, wherever it is, provided there is the inspiration of music, books, art. "I may sound like a recluse, but I'm not. I enjoy people, but when it comes to being social, I'm social only because I want to see certain people and share my house with them. I prefer a one-to-one relationship with guests, and that's how I feel about my house. I want to embrace it as a friend, not greet it like a distant stranger."

Ali MacGraw has brought an
aura of freshness and beauty to her
Malibu beach house.

LEFT: *Explaining that she "lives like
a nomad," the actress reveals her
gypsy spirit in a love of textiles,
including Living Room pillows
covered in Bakuba raffia cloth from
Africa, and a Tunisian rug.
Comfortable sofas, a canvas and
bamboo chair, and sisal carpeting
exemplify her preference for versatile
appointments that can accompany
her anywhere she may go.*

ABOVE: *For a Living Room still life,
Miss MacGraw, who catapulted to
fame in* Goodbye, Columbus,
*has chosen a Victorian silver frame
to set off a beguiling photograph of
her son, Joshua. Near the base
of a silver vase holding sprays
of flowers is a winsome Japanese
netsuke depicting lovers.*

ABOVE: *In a small Sitting Room, geometry animates woven and batik-patterned pillows and a Tunisian rug. A window reveals the ocean, which the actress loves for its "endless acres of privacy."*
OPPOSITE: *Plants and flowers punctuate the buoyant informality of the Dining Room. Etchings by Jody Baker offer an achromatic accent.*

PRECEDING PAGES: *Potted trees and flowers, in a landscape design by Hans Nagel, wreathe the Patio.* RIGHT: *Illustrating her dictum "Everything should be seen," the actress decorates the Master Bedroom with her jewelry and a Japanese silk kimono. Their color echoed by Garcia the cat, bamboo tables with a tortoiseshell finish flank the canvas-upholstered bed. Rugs, like the Turkish kilim, are often taken on trips, to re-create the atmosphere of home.* ABOVE: *A Georgian Irish teapot, bright with garden blossoms, joins treasures on a bedside table.*

PRINCESS MARGARET

Mustique is not yet quite part of the modern world. About half of it has become as tidy as any plantation, and perhaps the whole island will go that way, but now there is still some of the untamed Caribbean left—scrub, coral, coconuts, the sea beating against empty shores.

To bounce in a jeep up the rising and rutted earth track to Princess Margaret's house is to leave behind the island's few shops, its ramshackle jetty with one restaurant, and to return to uncleared land stoutly wooded with white cedars. It is an atmosphere evoking the eighteenth century. A pair of miniature square lodges with gates marks the approach to a house that suggests French pavilions and the sense of style combined with simplicity that has been known always as a hallmark of well-being.

Her Royal Highness The Princess Margaret has been a friend since childhood of Colin Tennant, who in 1959 bought Mustique and its 1400 acres from the Misses Hazell, descendants of a prominent English family on nearby Saint Vincent. When Princess Margaret married Lord Snowdon, Colin Tennant gave her as a wedding present a site on the southern end of the island. The only inhabitants then were the proverbial mosquitoes. Princess Margaret remembers that before the wedding Colin Tennant asked her, "Would you like a bit of my island? Or something I can wrap up and send you?"

Until the late 1960s nothing further was done about what is actually the one and only property that Princess Margaret owns in her own right—not actual Crown property. In the 1960s, however, the princess commissioned a design from the late Oliver Messel, noted theatrical designer and architect, who had had a leading role doing other houses on Mustique.

The land chosen by the princess is wonderfully open—on a headland of its own, with a steep drop down to sand-lined coves and lagoons on either side. No other house is to be seen, though Lord Litchfield has bought a plot to which there will be access through the same lodge gates leading to Princess Margaret's house. The view is extraordinary, a vast seascape encompassing several Grenadine islands — from Saint Vincent, Union and Carriacou to deserted Petit Mustique and variously rocky spits and spurs.

All this part of the archipelago was described by the writer Patrick Leigh Fermor in *The Traveller's Tree* as "hanging mysteriously in a blue dimensionless dream." And so it does. The position of Princess Margaret's house is its great attraction, to which all else has been subordinated. As the princess says, "Arriving here and looking around is always the greatest pleasure."

Oliver Messel set the whole house low, on a single floor, to make it unobtrusive. The main living room, occupying the breadth of the house, is flanked by two short wings comprising the four bedrooms and the kitchen, screened with flower beds and tropical plants and palms. To walk up the path to the entrance is, in effect, to be in a paved three-sided courtyard.

What might have been cramped has been raised by the pyramidlike roofs over the main living room as well as over the two small wings. The pitch of the roofs is attractively shallow, and their wooden shingles weather well, having acquired an antique patina in a very brief time. The double doors lead into the main room and then right through it to the garden, the architecture cleverly emphasizing the open air. Terraced steps descend to the swimming pool and to a gazebo thatched with palm branches. There the façade facing the sea is simple—light-colored neo-Georgian—brought together by a classically shaped, if flattened, pediment. A wide double door at the center is topped by a low fanlight.

"Once the building started," says Princess Margaret, "it went quickly. It was great fun to do, though I had to do it all from England. Oliver drew the house, but I said to him I was going to do the inside. I'd always longed to build a house—all one's own ideas about cozy corners."

Throughout, she has chosen what are the obvious hot-climate colors—whites and light blues—although her own bedroom is a vivid orange. Perhaps if Oliver Messel had been given more freedom, the house might have been rather more elaborate. Princess Margaret, however, had her own definite ideas and wishes to provide a livable setting, far from formality and grandeur.

H.R.H. The Princess Margaret welcomes the secluded simplicity of her Caribbean retreat on the tiny island of Mustique.
OPPOSITE ABOVE: *The U-shaped structure, conceived by the late set designer/architect Oliver Messel, is composed of a living room running the width of the residence and two flanking bedroom wings.*
OPPOSITE: *Double doors open to a vista of water and a canopy of sky.*
ABOVE: *In the Living Room, geometric-patterned flooring and a shaped and planked ceiling distinguish the minimal décor—a mingling of bamboo furniture, with Victorian plates offering brief touches of color.*

ABOVE: *A spectacular seascape is the unrivaled focus of the Living Room. Doors, folding back inconspicuously into deep reveals, open the room to the elements. Each doorway becomes a frame for a unique composition in blue.* OPPOSITE: *On the covered Terrace, cane-back chairs attend a sleek dining table enriched with* faux-*tortoiseshell stemware and armorial monteiths filled with flowers. A school of bottle-glass fish extends the marine leitmotif.*

ABOVE: *Beyond the swimming pool and a light screen of vegetation, islands of rock arise from the sea like great leviathans.*

OPPOSITE: *Gnarled branches penetrate the palm-thatched roof of a Gazebo at the edge of the headland. The chinoiserie railing offers an orderly contrast to the roof's rusticity. Waves break like white lace against the verdant shore. On the distant horizon, a stretch of land suggests primordial outcroppings within the vast expanse of sea and sky.*

ETHEL MERMAN

Most of us perceive entertainers as larger-than-life figures, and are correspondingly disappointed if we see that our heroes and heroines are in actuality pale shadows of their vibrant stage or screen personalities. This is emphatically not true in the case of Ethel Merman.

From the moment the door of her New York city apartment opens, one has no doubt of being in the presence of a legend, of a person gifted with almost superhuman vitality. "Where else could you find me but in New York?" she asks resonantly. "I've got everything here—the shops, my family, the theater."

She launches confidently into a description of her incredibly active way of life. "Now, look, we gals who live alone have learned one thing, and that's to hang on to the essentials. I'm no pack rat, and I know what I like. So, when I decided to move, I called the interior designer Carleton Varney—we're old friends—and I said, 'I want it comfortable, Carleton, and I want to understand it. I want a chair that looks like you can sit down on it.' Well, he's been through this three times with me, and he knows what I like. He's as down-to-earth as I am, and he never tries to impose anything on me. When I say, 'Carleton, I don't like it,' that's the end of it. But he does know I like a change now and then. Let's see, we've already been through three distinct periods in my bedroom colors. First it was all light blue; next it was black and yellow; then we went all out for red, white and blue. Now it's pink, white and green. I guess you could say that over the years I've mellowed somewhat!

"You see, I'm not a typical show-business person. I'm not knocking show people, but I just don't have many friends in the profession. I lead a very quiet life, and you don't see me party-going. Sure, I receive invitations, but I don't go. My private life is private."

Her professional life, however, has been one of constant activity—on the Broadway stage, side trips to Hollywood, appearances on television. But this glamorous career has left little mark on Miss Merman's domestic tastes. "Let me tell you, no apartment I ever lived in looked like a set from *Anything Goes*. Come to think of it, I don't even remember that set. I'm a theatrical person; I don't need bizarre backdrops."

Indeed, the star's cheerful lack of pretension is underscored by the contents of her present apartment. There are portraits, but they are by "amateur" friends such as Benay Venuta, rather than by professionals of the day. There are the awards reflecting her dynamic career, but they are tucked away in corners, as are the autographed likenesses of such luminaries as John and Robert Kennedy and Dwight D. Eisenhower, or the photograph of Miss Merman being presented to Queen Elizabeth II.

Her life has always been extremely mobile, and her answer to the problem of having to be ready to travel at the drop of a contract, and yet maintain the necessary comfort of a permanent home, is apartment-hotel living. This is a way of life almost unique to Manhattan, where many buildings are in effect apartments although providing hotel services. "This enables me to leave and not worry that the maid will have a nervous breakdown while I'm gone," says the singer in her straightforward way. The result, in Miss Merman's case, is an unaffected and fast-moving life, lived in rooms that are crisply designed to communicate her energetic pace.

"I think one reason Ethel and I get on so well is that she is such a forthright person," says Carleton Varney. "I adore her, but I don't idolize her. And she likes that." Miss Merman agrees: "When I have a problem, Carleton solves it." And she particularly appreciates his sensitivity to her day-to-day needs. "I can simply walk out of this apartment and know that it will all look as good as new when I come home from an exhausting tour. The colors will look just as fresh; I'll be surrounded by all my things; I'll feel the hum of the big city outside. What more could I ask of life? I'd rather travel than anything else, but only if I have all this to come home to."

Carleton Varney manages to sum up everything graciously: "A star is a star; she creates her own style and sets her own pace. All I had to do was choreograph a few of the steps." The imprint of Ethel Merman is a strong one, and it is strongly felt throughout her own domain.

Ethel Merman's Manhattan
apartment, designed for her by
Carleton Varney, offers a haven
from the high-powered pace of
a notable theatrical career.
A mix of strong color and the
repetition of a single floral fabric
infuse the Living Room with a
vivacity to match Miss Merman's
legendary vitality. An appropriate
highlight among the collection of
evocative artworks is Lady at the
Footlights by Edzard Dietz, above
the mantel. Accessories include a
needlepoint pillow made by Van
Johnson and a lively grouping
of Meissen musicians.

OPPOSITE: *Ethel Merman stitched the bright needlepoint pillows that accent the Library; Mary Martin did the rug canvas. Leaning against the wall are images of Miss Merman in* Annie Get Your Gun *and* DuBarry Was a Lady; *above them she is depicted as* Panama Hattie.
OPPOSITE ABOVE: *A Library ensemble mingles awards and a photograph of Ethel Merman with Queen Elizabeth after a Command Performance.*
ABOVE: *Victorian furnishings define Miss Merman's Bedroom.*

HENRY MOORE

The whitewashed asymmetrical front of Henry Moore's farm cottage probably has not changed very much in overall appearance since it was built in Elizabethan times. "Hoglands," says the artist with pride, "used to be a pig farmer's house. We have kept the old name." And pointing to the tall red-brick chimney, he says, "It is typical of the Tudor style." Although Much Hadham, some thirty miles northeast of London, was the birthplace of Henry Tudor, today this Hertfordshire village is much more celebrated for its "new" Henry.

The eminent artist explains that he and his wife, Irina, first visited Hoglands by chance during the air raids of 1940. Later, when his London studio was damaged, friends suggested he rent half of the farmhouse, which for centuries had been divided into two tiny dwellings for the use of local laborers. "The house was nearly falling to pieces," says Henry Moore. After a few years he was able to buy it.

Today the spirit of the interior of Hoglands is that of a personal and intimate minimuseum. The furniture is modest, the carpets and curtains simple, but the art is entrancing. The arrangement of the multitude of objects, ranging from large to minuscule, is unpretentious, almost haphazard.

The initial and overwhelming impression on entering the living room is that the number of visual objects distracts the eye. Among the hundreds of items are pebbles, papier-mâché eggs, Cycladic sculptures, African masks, pre-Columbian artifacts given to Moore by Diego Rivera, a French Gothic carving of a Madonna and Child, gourds, flints and a Medieval marble relief. The sculptor's taste is eclectic, but there is a sense that, aside from personal associations and memories, each of these objects is a lesson in sculpture for an artist who has spent his lifetime exploring shapes, textures, colors and materials. "I've always paid great attention to natural forms, to seashells, fossils, bones, tree trunks and eggs. I keep shapes of every sort around me to stimulate new ideas."

This sort of stimulation is immediately apparent in the surrounding buildings where Henry Moore practices his art. Directly to the right of the farm cottage there is an old stable, which served as his initial studio. Now called the "top studio," this skylighted room is where he finishes his smaller bronzes. Next to the finishing studio is the small etching studio, with an old five-spoked engraving press in the center. Henry Moore proudly says, "I've just finished thirty etchings here in two and a half weeks. I like to work morning, noon and night. Work is what one lives for."

Outside again, he points to a structure housing the Henry Moore Foundation. "I hope that after I'm gone, young sculptors will come to Hoglands to see how I worked." At the distant end of the property are located the large-sculpture studios and sheds.

"The garden used to extend just beyond this espaliered tree," explains Mr. Moore. His wife maintains the informal borders of shrubs, perennials and annuals, which curve with the trees and hedges. "Irina makes all the garden decisions. It is she who chooses the colors of the chrysanthemums in the fall and the places for the snowdrops in the spring."

In the yard between the studios, large bronze casts are being uncrated, and there is the bustle of activity everywhere. Assistants are translating one small plaster cast into a much larger polystyrene form. "Outdoor sculpture should be over lifesize, because outside space reduces an object in scale. I've always liked sculpture in the open air, and I like making pieces that stand in nature. Architecture has horizontal and vertical lines, but nature is asymmetrical. I'd prefer to have my sculptures shown in a natural setting rather than with the greatest architecture in the world."

Hoglands, and the land surrounding it, shows that Mr. Moore is as good as his word. He goes on to explain that he will place only two of his large sculptures in a great, thirty-acre expanse of meadow behind his studios. It is most important to him that the sheep continue to graze there. "I don't like sculpture parks and museums with large numbers of works. I think they nullify the whole point of sculpture and defeat the very thing you wanted them for." It is evident that Henry Moore has firm convictions about his art.

LEFT: *For forty years sculptor Henry Moore and his wife, Irina, have lived in their Elizabethan farm cottage, Hoglands, among a proliferating complex of studios.* BELOW LEFT AND BELOW: *"I'd prefer to have my sculpture shown in a natural setting rather than with the greatest architecture in the world," says Moore. Garden settings for his (left to right)* Draped Reclining Figure, Locking Piece *and* Oval with Points *reflect this feeling.* OPPOSITE: *Although the interior of the cottage has changed little over the years, the Living Room was a 1958 addition. Here Moore sits amid his very personal collection.*

LEFT: *An Anteroom announces the tenor of the residence, where works of art are integrated into deliberately simple and comfortable contexts.*
BELOW LEFT: *A Romanesque carving of a Madonna and Child mingles with a medley of forms in the unpretentious Living Room.*

OPPOSITE: *Henry Moore finishes his smaller bronzes in the skylighted brick-walled Top Studio. Here, alongside two casts of his* Upright Mother and Child, *1978, is a trio of little bronzes,* Three Bathers: After Cézanne, *1978. The airbrushed canvas that backdrops Moore's* Reclining Figure: Hand, *1976–78, enables the sculptor to study his work without architectural distractions.*

LEFT: *In the Open Plastic Studio is Moore's* Reclining Figure: Angles, *1977–79, in plaster.*
BELOW LEFT: *A 1975 bronze,* Three Piece Reclining Figure: Draped, *dominates the White Studio.*
BELOW: *Moore's small bathers reflect his admiration for the sculptural quality of Cézanne's figures. "Cézanne, for me, is most visual. He thinks three-dimensionally. I once said I could do models of all three figures of* The Bathers, *given this two-dimensional rendition by Cézanne," he says.*
OPPOSITE: *Working models and plasters in the White Studio reveal preliminary stages of Henry Moore's sculptural process.*

JEANNE MOREAU

In her country home, the glamorous image as stage and screen actress of international renown seems of incidental importance to Jeanne Moreau. Here, as a matter of fact, few things give her more pleasure than talking about the house itself, describing everything in it with affection. Indeed, for anyone—particularly for Mlle Moreau—the acquisition of a house is something of a love affair. And, like a love affair, there are the moments of decision and the moments of indecision.

Often a house is found by chance and admired by accident. It is put out of mind; it creeps back in; finally it becomes an obsession, impossible to resist. So it was with the actress and her retreat in the south of France near Saint-Tropez. Like all lovers, she is now in its thrall.

In 1961, after the great success of the film *Jules et Jim,* directed by François Truffaut, an exhausted Jeanne Moreau came south to rest in a quiet hotel in Saint-Tropez. Once refreshed, she was certain that she would be moving on again. "While I was at the hotel," she recalls, "some people who wanted to meet me telephoned and asked me to come to dinner. Frankly, I didn't really feel like it, but I accepted the invitation anyway. And so it turned out that I saw this house for the first time."

It is a large and peaceful dwelling, quite removed from the crowds and the busy life of Saint-Tropez itself. Not far from the sea, it is located in the hills outside of town, and the setting provides an atmosphere of calm, almost Alpine, dignity. In the distance can be seen the mountain range of the Massif des Maures, and on summer evenings the air is rich with the wild scents of the back country. Built in the early 1850s, the house is definitely part of the land and its heritage.

"You can see that I was already in love with the house the first time I saw it," says Mlle Moreau. "When I thanked my hosts that night and prepared to leave, I remember telling them to keep me in mind if they ever wanted to sell it. They weren't awfully pleased with that idea!"

Nevertheless, the image of the house lingered in her mind, and she found herself thinking about it from time to time. "I particularly remember one night in Paris after a dinner party. When the meal was over, Françoise Sagan came and sat next to me. She had a new card trick and insisted on telling my fortune with it. Then, after going through all the rigamarole with the cards, she announced solemnly, 'Death will bring a great wish of yours to pass.'

"Well, I didn't pay much attention—until a month or two later when I learned that, because of the recent death of the owner, the house in Saint-Tropez was for sale. So Françoise had been right, after all, and I hurried down to buy it. As it turned out, it took me four years to pay for it completely." And so the work of four years—the interpretation of many different and exacting roles on stage and screen—produced for her in the end a peaceful world of old stone walls and a white garden.

Surely this little world seems to represent what Jeanne Moreau has been looking for all her life: roots of her own and a safe anchorage. "My grandfather was an English sailor, you know, and I spent most of my childhood moving from one rented house to another in and around the port of Littlehampton, in Sussex. Now, even though I am not married, I have a tremendously nostalgic sense of a secure family life—a life, I suppose, I never had. For me this house has really become a family place."

Also, quite naturally, the house is filled with echoes of her acting career, and mementos of the films she has made. There is, for example, a rug woven by craftsmen in the small Brazilian village where she filmed *Viva Maria.* Nothing is contrived, however, and objects have been spontaneously placed by her own hand.

Unfortunately, the time has come for Jeanne Moreau to leave her house again—there is a film to be made, a play to be performed—and all the preparations and telephone calls tire her. For a moment her face clouds over like an autumn sky. She does not really want to leave Saint-Tropez. But then, realizing that she can always return to the house she loves, a marvelous smile breaks through, a smile of happiness, a smile with more than the radiance of a summer day.

ABOVE: *Jeanne Moreau became enamored of a country home near Saint-Tropez while on holiday after her remarkable performance in* Jules et Jim. *The house was only a tantalizing memory when Françoise Sagan predicted that the actress would fulfill a great wish; soon after, Mlle Moreau acquired the newly available house. Built in the 1850s, the residence embodies the charm of traditional French country architecture.*
OPPOSITE: *Beyond the garden, thickly wooded slopes unfold in the distance.*

ABOVE: *Reflecting Jeanne Moreau's desire for "a series of different levels,"*
the Library opens onto the spacious Living Room through balustraded
archways that echo gently arched windows. The drawing is by Picasso.
OPPOSITE: *Relaxed Living Room appointments evoke the warmth of country*
living. A large abstract painting by Rezvani resounds with the bright
essential colors of Provence. Mlle Moreau comments, "For me, this house
has become a family place, a place where my confidence can bloom."

ABOVE: In the Dining Room, a 19th-century English commode bears
gleaming testimony to delightful repasts shared with guests.
OPPOSITE: "I tried to preserve all the integrity and style proper to the
period in which the house was built," explains Jeanne Moreau. In the
Master Bedroom, antique tile flooring, rough-hewn beams and a door
adapted from an antique armoire exemplify this philosophy. The Venetian
commode was a gift from a dear friend, couturier Pierre Cardin.

PATRICIA NEAL AND ROALD DAHL

Some twenty-six years ago, when Roald Dahl and Patricia Neal were wintering in New York soon after they were married, Mr. Dahl's family wrote to him from England that a small Georgian house with five acres was up for auction in Great Missenden. He wrote back, asking them to try to get it for him. They bought it at auction in the village pub for £4,500. Mr. and Mrs. Dahl paid half of the total amount themselves and borrowed the rest from his mother.

They had become the owners of a small late-Georgian farmhouse with a slate roof, built around 1800. It had four square rooms downstairs and three upstairs, plus a bathroom. There was no heating other than a few fireplaces, and the kitchen—or what there was of it—had a floor made of huge uneven red tiles.

"For the next fifteen years," says Roald Dahl, "with the help of one of my best friends, Wally Saunders, a builder, and depending upon the money available, we worked to make the place pleasant and comfortable. We knocked down interior walls. We built an annex in the orchard. Later, we joined the annex to the main house; then we built onto the other side of the house." In the end there were six double bedrooms, three bathrooms, two living rooms, a dining room and a billiard room—and central heating. They built a greenhouse for Mr. Dahl's orchids and an aviary for parakeets and, finally, an indoor swimming pool. They tried their best to keep these additions as much as possible in character with the original house.

"In the next village, a large Rothschild mansion was being demolished," Roald Dahl recalls, "and from there, for almost nothing, we bought all the lovely Westmorland stone slabs from the cellars, as well as some immense stone steps that had led down to the Rothschild tennis courts. With all this, we laid out a terrace. In a niche in the wall at the end of the terrace, we placed a lifesize stone figure of an unknown English queen that had once graced the façade of the Houses of Parliament. And if you're wondering how I got *that*, I won't tell!

"I believe strongly that a garden should always—if you don't have a gardener—be designed to give maximum pleasure for minimum work. So I concentrated on species roses, floribundas and clematis. I hate weeding, so for ground cover on all flower beds I used Alpine strawberries, lilies of the valley and erica. I wanted some rhododendrons, but since we have a lime soil, I excavated one bed to a depth of six feet, lined the earth walls with corrugated iron, and refilled this hole with a different soil.

"But to go back indoors. I myself had become an enthusiastic collector of pictures as soon as World War II ended, in 1945. Each time I sold a short story I would buy a picture. Then, because it took me so long to write another story, I would invariably have to sell the picture I had bought six months before. In those days fine pictures were inexpensive. Many pictures that today could be acquired only by millionaires decorated my walls for brief periods in the late 1940s: Matisses, enormous Fauve Rouaults, Soutines, Cézanne watercolors, Bonnards, Boudins, a Renoir, a Sisley, a Degas seascape.

"After Pat and I had been married for a while, and when there was a bit more money in the bank, I began buying pictures for keeps. I admired Francis Bacon's work enormously, and we bought seven of his paintings. We also bought, for about £100 each, some superb eighteenth-century mirrors, and one is almost certainly by Mathias Lock.

"I then moved cautiously into the field of abstract painting—an early Moholy-Nagy, some Bombergs, a Klee. Then came a love affair with the great, but then virtually unknown, Russian painters of the early part of this century: Malevich, Rodchenko, Tatlin, Popova, Ermilov and the rest of them.

"My love of eighteenth-century English furniture is second only to my love of paintings. I don't admire anyone who buys fine furniture—or fine anything, come to that—without troubling to study the history of the artists involved. Equally, I don't admire those who buy only for investment. My pictures, which are now rather valuable, are not insured. If the house burns down, that's just bad luck. I would miss my pictures, but money would be no compensation."

English author Roald Dahl, master of the mischievous tale, and his wife, actress Patricia Neal, spent more than fifteen years restoring their Georgian farmhouse in Buckinghamshire, England. OPPOSITE: A French urn drolly crowns the entrance.

ABOVE: The Sitting Room testifies to the writer's passion for antique furniture and eccentric curios and paintings. Russian avant-garde art, including works by Malevich, Ermilov and Goncharova, distinguishes the collection; Liubov Popova's 1921 painting, left of the bay window, exemplifies the Constructivist aesthetic. The Oscar Patricia Neal won in 1963 for her role in Hud rests beneath it.

RIGHT: Translations of Mr. Dahl's books—including editions in Chinese and Swahili—occupy shelves in a Hallway. The Dutch still life is from the 16th century.

OPPOSITE ABOVE: *Intricate carvings in the style of Grinling Gibbons bracket a variety of artworks in the Sitting Room: a 17th-century religious panel; flanking it, a small Winston Churchill seascape and a Norwegian landscape; a Matisse drawing; and 19th-century English paintings.*
OPPOSITE: *Pheasants embellish the gilded tracery of an 18th-century mirror, a regal note in the Master Bedroom. An antique glass sphere, suspended from the ceiling, is meant to keep witches at bay.*
ABOVE: *A gaily painted Gypsy caravan summons enchantment to the garden. Enhancing the mood are the summer house and, hanging from a stately willow tree, an old-fashioned swing. The woods, glimpsed beyond the garden, endow the scene with tranquil beauty.*

MIKE NICHOLS

"I go into a coma when somebody starts showing me swatches. And when I wake up, having mumbled 'Yes, yes, that's fine' at everything, I may end up not liking what I've got. If that's the case, I just throw a rug over the offending object and live with it anyway!" It is clear that Mike Nichols is a man with his own ideas about interior design, and these ideas happen to correspond in a number of ways to the ironic and witty view of the world that is to be found in his work in the theater and in films.

For many years, as Mr. Nichols admits, being at home was not of much importance to him. "When you're young, it's great fun to spend the night in a twenty-four-hour restaurant and drive the waitress crazy by ordering two cups of coffee in six hours. But when you mature, your priorities change, especially when children become a focus in your life. Suddenly it's important to have the kind of place where friends can visit you, and where hitherto neglected arts, such as cuisine, may be practiced."

Luckily for Mr. Nichols the onset of this longing coincided rather neatly with his meeting Elinor Arnason, an interior designer whose work blends intelligence with discretion. "Elinor is easy for me to get along with," says Mr. Nichols. "She doesn't mind if I yell at her for having good taste." And he is unequivocal in his dislike of any surfeit of good taste. "I tend to get manic when I hear people talk about 'a really important piece' or 'a fun lamp' or 'just a dim whisper of a chiffonier,' and Elinor doesn't do anything like that at all. She just explains in simple language why I need a light in that corner."

As the result of a social encounter, Elinor Arnason was responsible for the design of Mr. Nichols's New York pied-à-terre and the rebuilding of a barn and the renovation of the main house on his country property.

"Whenever I acquire a new place to live," says Mr. Nichols, "I go into a mild panic. I'm suddenly acutely aware that I'm supposed to be 'expressing myself,' that my 'personality' must shine through everything. And I'm also aware that some people practice interior design as psychotherapy. 'If I redo my living room, I may become a whole new person,' that type of thinking. But it's rather important for me not to delve into myself, and I do want to live simply.

"In New York I was very insistent about having a view. It was a matter of a few good paintings, unobtrusive furniture and a huge order of skyline." This simple menu has, in fact, been translated into a simple and cool design for urban living with the help of Miss Arnason and the work of the architect Paul Krause. In the country, his needs were somewhat different, and the canvas was by no means as bare as it had been in New York. "When I started out, it seemed to me that New York would be a very transitory situation. And so it was—at first. But later I found myself spending more and more time in the city, with weekends and the summer being reserved for Connecticut." As a result, the atmosphere of the country house is decidedly informal. There is the impression of several layers of time, as well as of several distinct bands of taste, superimposed one upon the other.

Naturally, Mr. Nichols has changed, as his career has developed and grown more complex and demanding. "When Elaine May and I first started, we were in love with words. We loved to listen, to set up rhythms, catch their sparkle. I was always intensely verbal. And when I began to direct for the theater, I was really still dealing with a static world—or, at least, a world that was very controllable. In the theater everyone is on stage at the same time, and that's what makes it wonderful. In film, however, the same thing becomes deadly. That's why Chekhov is magical in the theater, boring on the screen. In film, one person counts, and it was through film that I became aware of visual things.

"Now I believe that, of all the senses, only the visual can be taught. You either have an ear for music, or you don't. But someone can come along and show me how a composition works on a certain canvas, and I'll remember it. Someone else will show me the source of light in a picture or a room or on a movie set—and I'll have *learned* that. Without being pompous, I can say that by becoming a film director, I really became much more aware of my physical environment."

New York

At home in his New York City apartment, as in his Connecticut country home, director Mike Nichols enjoys the traditional comfort of interiors designed for both residences by Elinor Arnason.

LEFT: *Dominating the Living Room is Balthus's large painting titled* Le Lever. *A Bessarabian rug defines the comfortable seating group composed of chairs covered in pristine cotton and a contrastingly earth-toned sofa sparked by light pillows. Tables bracketing the sofa bear a Marino Marini bronze figure (left) and an American folk art deer. Wall lamps illuminate the balanced symmetry of the décor.*

BELOW: *In the Guest Room/Sitting Room, Josef Albers's vigorous geometry counterpoints the delicacy of a David Hockney drawing.*

Connecticut

BELOW: *Dark shutters underscore the Colonial grace of Mike Nichols's clapboard country home, a peaceful oasis in rural Connecticut.*
RIGHT: *"I find myself responding to art as I do to friends," says Mr. Nichols. Artworks in the Connecticut Living Room echo the pastoral mood of the setting. A George Stubbs painting above the mantel suggests the director's avocation: raising Arabian horses. A vivid Bessarabian rug brightens the color scheme, while the lively patchwork of pillows and a quilt injects an air of gaiety.*

ABOVE: *Nature provides a lavish screen of verdure for an expanse of window on the Sun Porch. Sisal matting underlies the setting's clarity, spiced by wicker furniture upholstered in flower-strewn cotton. Antique accents include a wood-burning stove and a carousel horse.*

RIGHT: *Herring's painting of a horse and groom asserts the equine theme in the Library. The rug provides a unifying pattern, its hues repeated in the upholstery fabrics. A campaign desk serves literary endeavor.*

RIGHT: *The capacious barn of weathered cedar siding houses a screening room and guest facilities, which Elinor Arnason designed with architect Roland Dick.*

BELOW RIGHT: *Within the lofty Screening Room, a walnut table is the focus of a grouping enlivened by a medley of geometric fabrics. In another arrangement, Eames chairs on glides foster flexibility for ease of viewing. Nearby, a stairway ascends to balconied guest rooms.*

OPPOSITE: *Indigenous rocks and fieldstone ring the free-form swimming pool, a refreshing spot amid sheltering trees.*

CHRISTINA ONASSIS

One of the most challenging elements of an interior designer's work is to understand a client. When the client is as mobile as Christina Onassis, the situation is doubly complex. As Valerian Rybar explains it, logistics played a major part in the planning and subsequent execution of a large chalet in Saint Moritz for the busy young heiress. "Time was critical for both of us," the designer says. "Christina Onassis takes a very serious approach to her business interests, which are of course worldwide, and I myself have to think in terms of commuting between Paris and New York. So for both of us it was a question of finishing a complex project in the shortest possible time."

Six months is a remarkably brief span for such a project, but this was the time lapse from the day the first workman arrived to demolish the "not very attractive" interiors of the chalet, at that time ten years old. Irrelevancies, in the form of a red marble staircase and fussy balustrades, were swept away.

"We had hardly more than a handful of meetings," says the designer. "Christina Onassis is a person with definitive ideas about what she wants—and, more important, what she needs—in a winter home. Everybody forgets how young she is, and I wanted to express that fact in the house. It had to have a gregarious spirit, since she plans to do a great deal of entertaining over the coming years, and the house has to express a certain spirit that she has. She is very active in sports, especially when she is in Switzerland."

While Mr. Rybar admits that the assignment was a little more difficult than one in which he could have spent more time getting to know the owner of the house, the result of his concentrated labor is a work of unusual depth. It bears the imprint of the surrounding countryside in its rooms, and yet it is well suited to the luxurious and international way of life for which it was designed. The lavish yet paradoxically restrained effect of the chalet is achieved almost entirely through the use of natural materials. Woods of all kinds are used throughout—ranging from the native wood of Switzerland to the highly polished redwood plaque that serves as an abstract sculpture in Christina Onassis' bedroom.

Then there is wool. Used in all shades and textures, it serves to muffle an active life with its gentle and unassertive presence in room after room. Leather, sheepskin and suede have important roles to play, and the repertoire of organic materials even embraces such diverse substances as cork lining the study walls and the horn marquetry found on many pieces of the specially designed furniture. The massive use of stone serves to place at one with the mountain those structures that have drawn strength from it.

The house is a sturdy one, a fact that pleases both owner and designer: "Christina Onassis is a practical person," says Mr. Rybar, "and she understands that in a chalet there is little point in using antique furniture. And so, apart from a few objets d'art, there isn't any."

Underneath the sumptuous façade of Valerian Rybar's work there is an entirely functional imperative: "The people I work for are busy, but they appreciate comfort. And that really is what luxury is all about today. If you can give someone a completely covered and heated access to the garage and to the ski equipment, as I have done here—well, I think that's almost as important as giving them the most extravagant and delectable living room. Attention to detail is also very important to me, as it is to Christina Onassis. There are little nuances in this house that some people will not understand—references to local art and traditions. But the critical thing is that they exist. By their presence they imply scholarship, and they add a certain depth to the work. Design doesn't stop at the door of the china cupboard, and this assignment was truly a complete project. Everything down to china and linen was brought into the house for its first season."

Perhaps the fullest understanding and appreciation of the chalet may be gained by considering it not as the plaything of an international figure, used only for a few weeks a year, but as the sophisticated version of a somewhat traditional story. It is the story of the perpetual traveler finding a haven at last in a beautiful and hospitable country of lakes and mountains.

When designer Valerian Rybar renovated a chalet in Saint Moritz for Christina Onassis, he modified the exterior to reflect local Swiss tradition; inside, he reconciled discreet practicality and refined comfort.

OPPOSITE AND ABOVE: The Living Room is luxuriously detailed in a restrained contemporary mode. Wool, in subdued tones, is used extensively— for walls and draperies, carpeting and sofas. The snow-covered splendor of the Corvatsch Mountains is a magnificent backdrop for a plaque of petrified wood. Above the fireplace is a painting by Dubuffet.

ABOVE: *A warming fire, the vivid color scheme, and rustic paneling and beams increase the informal lodgelike atmosphere of the small Dining Room. A giant bronze fish seems to float above the massive oak table, while a 16th-century English wooden bowl trimmed with nailheads adorns the overmantel. Under candlelight, pewter adds a lustrous gleam.*
OPPOSITE: *A wool-upholstered banquette and large leather-covered chairs are grouped for easy conversation in the Study. A mural, painted in the Gothic manner, depicts the view visible through a living room window.*

LEFT: *A Hallway leading to the master suite and guest rooms is distinctively defined by carved and painted Arven wood that was patterned after the woodcarving of Switzerland's Engadine region.*
BELOW LEFT: *Painted Alpine flowers on the Arven-wood moldings in the Boudoir re-create a delicate and traditional motif.*
OPPOSITE: *A large redwood plaque resembles an abstract sculpture against a Master Bedroom wall upholstered in suedelike cloth. Sensuous textures complete the restfully snug setting.*

ZANDRA RHODES

"I love objects for themselves. I'll see a vase and use it for flowers, even if it is not going to stand up very well. I'll place a table just where you'll always bump into it if I believe it looks *good* there. Getting across a room in my place is like running an obstacle course."

Zandra Rhodes, British fashion designer, moves from one convenient seat, a full, lidless trash can near the stove, to another, a twenty-foot banquette. There she flops onto fluffy cushions of salmon-pink and white satin, quilted and piped in gold. Both perches are appropriate as opposing images of the Rhodes residence. Hers is a five-floor house in a London square, of faded Victorian grandeur, now seedy and with stucco peeling. The place wears a dowdy coat outside, but lift the hem—and behold within a wondrous and colorful and quite unique dream house.

Zandra Rhodes is famous for the clothes she makes: her own designs and dyes worked into cloudlike creations of chiffons, jerseys, frills. Wear one, and you step into the beautiful dreams of make-believe. Many claim she is the world's most original dress designer. The word often used in connection with her work and her personal appearance is *fantastic.* And her home is in quite the same spirit. Much of it spills over with strange and eccentric glamour, and more remains unrendered, with work in progress. The house is characteristic of the owner: casual in jeans and plastic sandals, or bedecked in butterfly-wing colors, shimmering like an opal.

She herself is an art form. "My problem," she explains, "is that I'm totally dominated by my work. I love it. I cannot divide my surroundings from my work and, if I were at home during the week, it would be traumatic. I couldn't concentrate. As a rule, I try to leave here in the morning no later than 7:25.

"The arrangement of objects doesn't bother me. If I'm sleepy, I don't even move the mountain of cushions off the bed. I'll sneak along the edge and fall asleep, rather than disturb them."

Part of the Rhodes thinking can be seen in the incredible entrance hall and stairs. "We did a quick facial job on it," she says, leaning against a towering column of mirror mosaics. She explains how she invited a work force of ten friends for brunch and decorating. Pots of paint were opened; stepladders and mops were made ready. On arrival, each friend was presented with a cup of coffee and a sponge of one-color paint. Thereupon a day of sponge pointillism began, and the end results are an emulsioned wall of considerable imagination and a ceiling of many different and attractive colors.

The original layout for the rooms was worked out in collaboration with American party-set designer Richard Holly. He created the plastic urns filled with fir cones, white coral and dried flowers. He also designed her shop interiors, and says of their work together: "Zandra is more talented, more creative and more personal than any ten ordinary people. But to carry out the interior design, she still needs the discipline of professionally qualified advice. The lesson I learned was how to take elements from her work and reinterpret them for the house."

And her theatrical house has several special needs. "The main purpose," says Zandra Rhodes, "is having somewhere to entertain my friends." She dodges a make-believe cactus crafted of green pleated satin. "Friends are inspirational, but often they ask how I can stand living as I do, surrounded by expressions of my work. They themselves need to get away from theirs to unwind. But I *must* have this extension of myself. So the house, like a garment, is a second skin."

Isolated from her home, she claims to feel lost: "Out of my context, I feel a horrible gnome. Once my friend Billy Al Bengston rented a whole beach in Mexico and we sat there for three days. I felt like an ant. If I try to go sporty, well, I'm not much good at it. So, like my makeup, the house really must be a mask. I'm trapped into being a star and being stared at. But I like it. At this stage I've proved myself, yet I think many good designers suffer from an inferiority complex inside."

Her long-term aim is to live both in her London house and in an enormous New York loft. "Or an old cinema, or a huge warehouse! But best of all, I suppose, would be some glorious 2,000 square feet of entirely open space."

The Living Room of British fashion
designer Zandra Rhodes's Victorian
townhouse in London abounds with
expressions of her creative spirit:
unique satin print fabrics, a
twenty-foot banquette, a backless
serpentine sofa and playful
satin-wrapped wooden cacti.
American designer Richard Holly,
who collaborated on the interior
design, created the ingenious
Z-shaped table and the fir-cone
forms in plastic urns.

ABOVE: *A view of the Living Room work area reveals a drawing board, a collection of painted cardboard boxes and the unusual pottery of Carol McNicoll. Fresh lilies and an amyrillis offer a contrast to the playful fake organic forms.*

OPPOSITE: *"Footlights" glamorize the sleeping area of the Living Room, a space that will eventually become a guest suite. Surreal painted columns partition the area; the lavish tenting and painted floor provide exotic texture.*

OPPOSITE: *The tiny half-landing Bath alcove is draped with vivid vinyl and patterned felt. Within this complex mise-en-scène, the reflection of a mural by Martin Sharp suggests the backdrop of a stage set.*
ABOVE: *A polystyrene Mexican statue on a concrete ziggurat, and an Inca-style carving atop a painted brick wall, transform the little back garden of Zandra Rhodes's townhouse into a mythic retreat.*

FRANÇOISE SAGAN

Some twenty-five years ago, at the age of eighteen, Françoise Sagan created an international reputation with her avant-garde novel, *Bonjour Tristesse.* In the years that followed, other novels—like *Un Certain Sourire* and *Aimez-vous Brahms?*—have appeared in modest profusion, along with plays and films, and today Mlle Sagan is one of France's best-known writers. Her literary themes are often concerned with the young and the innocent and their search for experience. Many times, in her books, that search results in disillusionment, at once despairing and cynical, and she has a masterful way of describing those final events that are so tinged with melancholy—the end of an affair, the last days of summer, the subtle but irrevocable transitions that mark permanent change.

As is the case with many writers, the world she inhabits is largely one of the imagination. However, she does bring to her personal life much of the casual bohemian charm and quasi-existentialist thrust of her work. In point of fact, she is a kind of immovable nomad, and carries to each of her homes a private sensibility that never seems to change. As a result, the houses in which she lives, both in Paris and in the country, share the same unique charm.

"Perhaps it's because I don't really worry much about them," says Mlle Sagan in partial explanation. She is in her Paris house, sitting in the large upstairs studio that she has chosen for her bedroom. A rather harsh light illuminates the velvet armchairs; an indoor poplar tree reaches toward the high ceiling; and lying on the rug is her German shepherd, Werther, who hardly ever leaves her side.

When asked whether she finally feels at home, after some dozen moves within Paris itself over the last twenty years, she smiles. "Yes, I think so, and perhaps the reason is that I often find myself enjoying a wonderful solitude here." The delightful house that, after so many nomadic years, she finally discovered in Paris has a definite provincial flavor. It is, indeed, reminiscent of her country house in Normandy, and it almost seems as if the *Manoir du Breuil* has been in some way transported intact to a Parisian district that is largely inhabited by artists and craftsmen.

Françoise Sagan is always delighted to talk about her country house at Equemanville in Normandy—and particularly how she came to acquire it. "The house itself was built around the turn of the century, and the first time I saw it, I was immediately taken with it. I leased it on the spot—a marvelous place to rest and to watch the sea, and where I could invite my friends." The owner, seeing such enthusiasm, was anxious to sell her the château, but she resisted the idea. He was persistent, and he finally won out—in a rather mystical way.

It happened to be August 8, 1968, and the number 8 figured prominently in the price wanted for the house. In fact, the night before, Mlle Sagan had won exactly the required number of francs at the gambling tables of Deauville. What gambler worthy of the name could have resisted the number 8 coming up three times in a row? It was inevitable that her casino winnings served to buy the château, and she instantly became the owner. It was one of those apparently irrational gestures that abound in her life and serve to keep Mlle Sagan eternally young.

In any event, it is more to the point to describe, not so much the houses in which the famous writer lives, but rather the way she lives *in* them. Feeling diffident about being a chatelaine, she seems to prefer the role of invited guest in her own home. A certain reluctance to own possessions, coupled with a charming indolence and a love of the unexpected, prevents her from giving herself over completely to being a homeowner. By way of illustration, she is never exactly certain who might be staying in the country house or when someone is expected, and a housekeeper looks after the needs of her many guests.

However, though she may lack some of the possessiveness of a homeowner, her houses mean a good deal to her. The country house, for example, is essentially a huge green bed into which she can tumble and recharge her energies. And, in a curious and intriguing way, it is almost exactly like her house in Paris. Both of them are private worlds, expressions of her imagination.

Paris Townhouse

At home in Paris, Françoise Sagan
enjoys both solitude and conviviality.
Here, and at her Normandy country
house, the French writer lives—alone
or among her many friends—with
a casual abandon that recalls the
mischievous character Cécile in her
novel Bonjour Tristesse.
LEFT AND ABOVE: "I would almost
prefer to live in the garden itself,"
Mlle Sagan says of her Paris
residence, "but it's so small that
you nearly fall right into the
fountain." She often welcomes
and entertains her guests here.

With existential aplomb, Mlle
Sagan has unified her environments
by giving the Paris house the same
sort of relaxed provincial feeling as
the country house—in part by
interchanging the furnishings.
OPPOSITE: In the Paris Salon,
comfortable chairs cluster close to
the Directoire marble fireplace. The
nude, at left, is by Louis Picard.
OPPOSITE BELOW: Mlle Sagan's
Bedroom, a large chamber reached
by a steep staircase, is her quiet
refuge. Canvases lining the walls
are all works that have piqued
the writer's imagination.
LEFT: A small Jardin d'hiver
projects a cheerful greenhouse
atmosphere. The trumeau and
console are late 19th century.

Normandy Château

OPPOSITE: *Built circa 1900, Mlle Sagan's Equemanville château, the*
Manoir du Breuil, was in disrepair when the writer purchased it with
the exact number of francs she had just won at the Deauville casino.
TOP: *An* allée *of beech trees forms an impressive natural entrance canopy.*
ABOVE: *Typical Norman half-timbered architectural detailing lends*
distinction to the tile-floored Entrance Hall.
TOP RIGHT: *A large open fireplace is the dominant feature in a Small Salon.*
ABOVE RIGHT: *Rush-seated chairs join a Victorian settee in the Large Salon.*

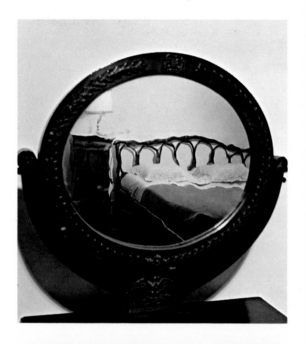

LEFT: *In another Small Salon, a marble mantel and an Italian giltwood mirror, both 18th century, enrich the countrified setting.*
OPPOSITE: *A round Directoire dressing mirror reflects a somewhat surreal glimpse of the 19th-century twig-motif bed that Mlle Sagan acquired locally for her Bedroom.*
OPPOSITE BELOW: *Floral chintz and a verdant view enliven one of several Guest Rooms the writer has arranged for her visitors.*

ARNOLD SCAASI

"I don't know what to do with this house, it's so awful," groaned Arnold Scaasi at the first sight of his shingled summer retreat, a vast affair facing a tranquil Quogue inlet. That said, within three short months he turned it into one of Long Island's most delightful houses. The ponderous frame structure—with dozens of small rooms clustered around the central living hall's massive brick fireplace and broad staircase—had, to give it its due, a certain Henry Jamesian charm. But the house needed modern logic and discipline to clear up its antiquarian confusions.

Fashion designer Scaasi had already had one Victorian summer house, and he did not want the same look again. So enclosing elements were condemned, walls fell—in fact, the whole house might have fallen, had a steel column not been introduced at a crucial point—doors went, windows were moved or enlarged, a few acres of glass let the outside in, and woodwork and ceilings were lacquered in assertive colors. Everything was transformed, driving shafts of light through the old house's dark eclectic heart.

Comfort, of course, had a top priority in Arnold Scaasi's plan. "I'm very against houses in the country where you rough it," he says emphatically. "So when I rebuilt this one, it was not to make myself *less* comfortable than I am in town. I come here to relax and enjoy myself thoroughly." Nevertheless, Mr. Scaasi would "rather live in one attractive room than in twenty that are unattractive."

But here in Quogue all twenty rooms are attractive, inviting, alive with light and color. The colors, in fact, are now relentless, and delight in their cheerful lack of restraint. The stairwell and hall are unequivocally tangerine orange—a hue copied from a favorite pair of beach shorts. The color contrasts dynamically with yellow doors and the stairs' handsome white balustrade.

On summer evenings the house is often filled with guests, and the flow tends to spill out onto the terraces and sloping lawns between house and inlet. From outside, every room can be seen at once: the hall, the bedroom, the upstairs sitting room, the green bath, the dining room. Seen from the garden or bay at night, the house has the playful and thoroughly enchanting look of a giant doll's house. A whimsical collection of big, bright fiberglass balls by sculptress Grace Knowlton, strewn across one end of the lawn, brings the varied house colors out onto the uniform natural green of the grass. An unexpected relationship is established between outside and inside that is poetic, imaginative—and, most important, just good fun.

Inside, the dining room has become the heart of the house. In the beginning Mr. Scaasi found a large gloomy room with plate rails, beamed ceiling and a tiled fireplace. He opened up one end with a broad window moved from the old living room, stripped the walls and fireplace of their period ornaments, lacquered the woodwork and beams white. He papered it, ceiling and all, in a blue and white print that matches the upholstery; the table skirts and napkins are also in the same blue and white fabric.

"The whole point is to be able to change it, which is an idea I have about dining rooms," says Arnold Scaasi. "And I feel very strongly about tables. Tables should show great fantasy. Forks can be orange, knives white, soup spoons blue, dessert spoons yellow. I use whatever I have for a centerpiece. Almost anything can decorate a table—radishes, lemons, a watermelon."

There are always lots of simple flowers placed everywhere around the house. "Daisies and geraniums look good in the country," says the owner. Along with these, the house is stocked with a very personal collection, including both excellent modern art and "things" found locally. They all eventually find their proper place. A Hosiasson painting over the fireplace was the only thing that came and just stayed put. Everything else is far less rigid. Some mirrored Mexican plant stands make lamp bases; there is a splendid Lucas Samaras box; a ball covered with guinea fowl feathers, found in a yard sale; a Sam Francis painting; two souvenir photograph frames from the Alhambra, in Granada; some painted Austrian porcelain ducks from London; Mexican and Moroccan rugs and Indian embroideries. All are part of Arnold Scaasi's strategy for a thoroughly comfortable country life.

Fashion designer Arnold Scaasi architecturally restructured his Victorian retreat, on Long Island, to create an open flowing plan with a distinctive contemporary look. RIGHT: *Modern art basks in light in the crisp and airy Living Room. The painting above the fireplace is by Hosiasson; the canvas behind Dubuffet's free-standing sculpture is by Boris Fedushin. Whimsical "feet" descending the stairs are also by Dubuffet.*

OPPOSITE: *Another view of the cheerful Living Room reveals more of the unusual wedge-shaped banquettes and ottomans Mr. Scaasi designed. The framed sculpture behind the mercury lamp is the work of Lucas Samaras.*
RIGHT: *From an upstairs Sitting Room, a sweep of shore reiterates the superb location of the house.*
BELOW: *Affectionate 19th-century Austrian porcelain ducks, artless daisies and handpainted "fish" place mats add character to a table set for dinner in the vividly patterned Dining Room.*

215

LEFT: *Mr. Scaasi's choice of color for the Hall was inspired by a favorite pair of beach shorts; he dramatically defined the hot hue with stark light trim. The reflective lacquer of the ceiling adds a sense of height. "The yellow doors," he explains, "simply looked good opening into the bedrooms." The abstract painting is by Alice Baber.*

ABOVE: *The soft-toned Master Bedroom provides a respite from the unrestrained color used elsewhere. A Dubuffet gouache stands near the bed. A 19th-century bamboo screen effectively serves as a headboard.*

BOBBY SHORT

One of the most subtle and elusive feats of interior design seems to be the creation of a successful environment for a famous individual. All too often the result is either so personal and crammed with mementos of a brilliant career that it serves to intimidate, or it is chillingly neutral, studiously avoiding anything other than international cliché. Pianist and singer Bobby Short has sidestepped both these pitfalls, orchestrating nine rooms in a rambling Victorian building in Manhattan into an original and authentic reflection of his own personality.

"First of all, you should know that my feelings about this apartment are bound up with my attitude toward the city," says Mr. Short. "I call it 'surviving attractively.' Much of my fascination with New York has always been to observe the ability of people to survive, to overcome all the obstacles this city throws in their path, and then go on from there to fashion an elegant and well-ordered life in spite of it all."

Among the rooms that are eloquent paradigms of Bobby Short's observations is the music room, occupying what at earlier stages in the apartment's history served as a living room. A gleaming lacquered piano dominates the space, echoed by a faultless wall of mirrors. It is a perfect statement of the singer's interests and, at the same time, a metaphor for his own suave public persona. The library is equally expressive of another side of Bobby Short's personality. It is filled with books that are unmistakably the collection of a man with wide interests outside the usual gilded wavelength of show business. In addition, there are straw baskets and stools from Africa, paintings and drawings that relate to Mr. Short's own career, and objects of all kinds from many different countries.

"I am a collector," says the musician, with the air of one confessing to an unfashionable vice. "But I'm struggling against the impulse. It's just that wherever I go, I find things that I like. One solution—but not a very good one—would be to pack everything away so I would have the things without having to look at them!"

Each room in Bobby Short's apartment seems to reflect a different aspect of him: the muted glamour of the music room, the highly personal library and an unsentimental dining room, filled with natural and transparent details. The kitchen, reflecting yet another facet of his personality, is disarmingly cozy, with wide-planked floors and deliberately naive details.

Preferring his own company and that of a few close friends to the stereotyped round of parties and discotheques, Mr. Short maintains a definite air of rationality and order in his life, reflected both in his long allegiance to the Café Carlyle—where he has performed for over ten years—and in his apartment. "There is one distinction that I make, and that is between professionals and dilettantes. I think there are few of the latter who are really successful at being decorative. You see, I admire people who have a *plan.* I think it's the most important thing in the world, and shaping your own ideas and tastes into a cohesive design is a wonderful challenge. In terms of the interiors in this apartment, I've tried to achieve a sense of relaxation without sacrificing an underlying discipline."

At the suggestion that this is perhaps akin to what he strives to do in his singing, Bobby Short pauses and then replies, "I was discussing this with an architect recently, and he claimed there was a great deal of similarity between a design and a song. I told him music is a good deal more ephemeral—in spite of recordings. But we did finally agree on certain basic points: the need for balance, moderation and coloration.

"There is another important point I'd like to make: It is a privilege to own beautiful things, but I don't believe that possessions should be treated with kid gloves. Lovely things should never be abused, but they should be *used,* not treated as precious embalmed objects. Of course, I realize that one day someone else will own them. Once you've faced the music, as it were, and accepted your own mortality, it can be rather fascinating to speculate just who the next owner might be! In the meantime, I'm philosophical about transcience and loss. I value my friends more than furniture or objects." In Bobby Short's life design, it is clear, meaningful relationships form a dominant theme.

Bobby Short's sophisticated music
has long been a magnet for
Manhattan café society night life at
the Hotel Carlyle. Like his music,
the apartment designed by the
entertainer communicates gracious
ease within a well-ordered context.
ABOVE: Richard Merkin's portrait
makes a strong statement in the
Entrance Hall. The handcarved
walking sticks are from Ethiopia.
RIGHT: An Indian challis throw
warms the Living Room sofa, while
the Music Room, mirrored in the
background, is enlivened by a
New Guinea ritual-house pole. The
painting is by Ronaldo de Juan.

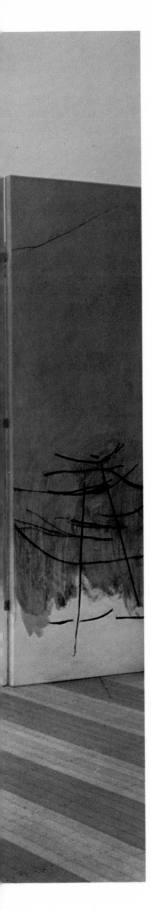

LEFT: *A distinctive bleached wood floor and an unusually high dado establish a linear architectural framework in the free-flowing Dining Room. A paneled folding screen, painted by Ronaldo de Juan, adds calligraphic punctuation. Within this light, uncluttered space, a focus of interest is a collection of brass and wood candlesticks massed on the sleek, glass-topped dining table. Mies van der Rohe cane and chrome dining chairs extend the room's spare atmosphere.*

ABOVE: *Recycled barn siding gives a warm feeling to the Kitchen, with its nostalgic collection of theater posters and ethnic memorabilia.*

RIGHT AND BELOW RIGHT: *Paintings by Richard Merkin enrich one wall of the comfortable Library. Another wall is devoted to extensive collections of books, records and small objects. Standing rigidly at attention in the background, a statue of a Moroccan palace guard injects a gentle note of humor.*
OPPOSITE: *A tailored purity infuses the Master Bedroom, designed by Chris Parker. The mirrored headboard wall amplifies the setting. At right is a de Juan lithograph, and, at left, a West African goat head carving.*

BARBRA STREISAND

"Ever since I can remember, I've had an instinct for decoration," says Barbra Streisand. "I can remember my first apartment in New York—it was a railroad flat on Third Avenue—and how I filled it with screens and lacquered chests. Even when I had no money, there was always the need to transform my surroundings." That gift for turning eccentricity into beauty, unevenness into richness, and originality into fashion was a hallmark of the early Streisand years, and it still forms a vital part of her appeal.

But the idiosyncratic and personal record of her New York years—and, in many ways, the fitting climax of them—is the duplex she bought some twelve years ago in an eccentric and uneven part of Manhattan, the very Upper West Side. Typically, with her great sense of self-anthology, the singer has it still. The duplex has a wonderful perch in a steeply raked Art Déco building, with an exposed and windy and very fine view of Central Park.

"Look, this was my first real home," Miss Streisand explains in her urgent voice. "Let me tell you, I wanted Louis, Louis, Louis—as much as I could lay my hands on. And I got it: bronzes, porcelains, satin, moiré. Later I became far more sophisticated."

The main illustration surviving from the Streisand Rococo period is the living room. It is an unexpectedly restrained and delicate space, with none of the overtones of excitement and color that must have been part of its owner's life at the time she conceived it. "It's all so interesting to me now," she says, with a possible note of irony in her voice. "I've moved so far away from this room, the politeness of it all, the conventionality. But I didn't make the connection, realize the necessity of setting up a link between who you think you are and the way you live."

That came later, in rooms such as the library. "My burgundy era," sighs Miss Streisand, "and the beginning of my breakaway from dollhouse taste. I was discovering the pleasures of Victorian and Second Empire furniture, and becoming a little daring—like covering the armchairs in a pink herringbone fabric. But even this was a beginning of the reversion to a truer self.

"When I made my debut at the Bon Soir at the age of eighteen, I wore a severe little Victorian blouse with a high black collar. The next day the reviews took as much notice of what I was wearing as they did of my singing. I was a little intimidated, and I didn't want anyone to think I was using my clothes as a gimmick. I suppose it was the same with this apartment. It took me a little time to be able to come out into the open and honestly say, 'This is me, Barbra, and this is what I like.' Today, of course, I think effects should be subtler. And this philosophy is apparent in other areas of my life as well. By the way, when I mentioned clothes, I realized that I seldom think about interiors I've created without a sort of backward glance at my wardrobe. Clothes and the environment you live in. How can you really separate them?"

Of course, it is in the nature of owning things to want more—to make collections complete, to round out and fill in. And so the game continues. "Sometimes I long for a Moroccan house, all white walls and practically no furniture. Then I come to my senses. I remember how much I like burgundy, and what I feel about the future of maroon. I never deliberate about what I like. To me the act of making a choice is an emotional experience, not an intellectual one."

As it is for any collector, the integrity of her world is important to the singer: "It drives me crazy to find that there's a leak in the ceiling, or that some of my things are moldering away in storage. I guess at heart I'm a compiler of inventories." And then she tells of her latest project: "I would like to document everything I own— every pair of shoes, every antique fan, all my jewelry and objects. I'd like to have it all photographed and bound in volumes." Miss Streisand might not be aware that she is emulating Queen Victoria of England, who had thick albums recording all her possessions in all of her palaces. Soon, indeed, Miss Streisand, with her multiplying number of California homes, may rival the late queen in sheer numbers of residences. For the moment, however, she is far above the busy streets of New York—quite at home and extraordinarily contented in her own private world.

ABOVE: *In Barbra Streisand's Manhattan duplex overlooking Central Park, the Entrance Hall features a traditional balanced arrangement in which a pair of Venetian chairs demurely flank a French Victorian console. The antique Italian portrait provides an arresting focal point.*
OPPOSITE AND FOLLOWING PAGES: *Formality and soft-toned restraint characterize the Living Room, unified by the gentle hues of an Aubusson rug; glass-topped tables reveal the rug's graceful patterns. Applied wall moldings allude to period paneling. Silk draperies, harmonious upholstery fabrics and a profusion of flowers extend the subtle palette.*

TOP: *In the Library, Art Nouveau and Art Déco collections include French bronze candlesticks, art glass and a sculpture of dancer Loie Fuller.*
ABOVE: *Miss Streisand refers to the Library décor as her "burgundy era." The rich hue underscores Grammys and an Oscar, visible at left. The large painting over the sofa is by Jason Monet.*
RIGHT: *The Dining Room is highlighted by a sumptuous table setting with an Irish linen cutwork cloth. The still life is Flemish.*

RIGHT AND BELOW: *Miss Streisand's Edwardian-style Bedroom is a delicate bower wherein the repetition of a single floral-patterned fabric instills unity and an aura of romance. Appliquéd bed undercurtains enhance the mood with diaphanous grace; a child's antique dressing gown crystallizes the feminine feeling. A carpet-clad platform visually separates the sleeping area from an inviting conversation grouping.*

MR. AND MRS. HAL WALLIS

Up the coast from Santa Monica, California, is an area that is little known and still has a feeling of quiet isolation. Even its name, Trancas, does not suggest long days of languid luxury—not in the way Santa Barbara, Emerald Bay and La Jolla summon up images of the good life in the sun. Trancas could be any sort of place. It is, however, an unspoiled area of California where a handful of people live privately at the beach. Life here revolves around the ocean, and from the street all that can be seen of any particular house is perhaps a garage and a noncommittal fence, one not much different from another. So it is with this Trancas house, but inside the gate the world becomes an entirely different and unique place.

Martha Hyer, actress and wife of film producer Hal Wallis, says, "Our haven is here; it's like paradise." Grape ivy climbs over an arbor, daisies in planters seem almost wild in their long-stemmed bravado, and there is a patch of bluegrass. Someone says, "Bluegrass at the beach? Impossible!" But, tended with care, the grass is thriving—a happy collaboration between Mrs. Wallis and landscape architect Harvey Wallace Kinnear.

Inside, the house opens to the air and the sea and the sand, white and uncluttered. There is a feeling of seclusion, perhaps from the thick trees that shield it from the neighboring houses, perhaps from the dunes capped in flowering ice plant, or from the quiet expanse of sand and air. "When I'm in town," says Mrs. Wallis, "I say to myself that at the beach I'm going to write letters and do all sorts of things. But when I get here, I end up doing very little but resting and being with my husband. We enjoy the sunset and perhaps a fire before dinner."

Mr. Wallis himself, producer of such classic films as *Casablanca*, is quick to agree: "I love the warmth, simplicity and comfort." It is easy to see why. There are daisies and geraniums, brass and copper and the soft sheen of polished wood, baskets and earthenware, denim and linen. And everywhere there are happy memories.

Mr. and Mrs. Wallis rented a house for several summers before deciding to buy, then spent another summer in a house next door, watching the remodeling. It literally started from the ground up, and all that was left of the original structure was the foundation. Today it has become a home of deep personal meaning.

Working on details with architect Harold Levitt, Mrs. Wallis conceived its design with the instinct and sensitivities of a woman who has her priorities well in order. "When friends came to visit during the construction," she says, "some would say, when they saw the kitchen, 'Oh, you're not going to have any privacy. The cook will be right there when you're entertaining.' And I said, 'I'm the cook.' And I love being here cooking and watching people sitting around the fire having a drink. I put food out on the long bar, and people help themselves and then sit around the table. It's warm and pleasant."

The sun has shifted, lending the sky a rosy afternoon glow. A bowl of apples rests on the table, shells gathered from the beach circle a wooden plate holding a potted geranium, and Early American quilts are framed on the wall. It is a house that nourishes the senses, makes no demands, offers pleasures at every turn.

"Although this beach house is clearly an expression of our taste and a personal illustration of what Hal and I like," says Mrs. Wallis, "I could not have done it without the help of Margot Tennant, who owns the Tennant Galleries. She gave me a great deal of direction and inspiration, and she is a dear friend. It's all worked out so very well. Sometimes I just love to sit here and look at the blue and white spongeware, the wire baskets, the candle molds. Then I like to look out at the ocean."

Mr. Wallis himself is every bit as enthusiastic as his wife; it is clear that he relishes the peace and relaxation and the lack of the usual pressures of a film producer's life. "I'm more than pleased with everything Martha has done here," he says in confirmation. Indeed, the locale and the house are so very peaceful that it is difficult to believe that the great city of Los Angeles—and Hollywood itself—lies not many miles away. Quoting Anne Morrow Lindbergh, Mrs. Wallis says, "This house is our own gift from the sea.'"

Film producer Hal Wallis and his wife, actress Martha Hyer, enjoy the serenity and comfort of their oceanside retreat in Trancas, California. ABOVE AND LEFT: Set back from the street is a thriving bluegrass lawn and a grape ivy arbor that leads to the country-style entrance. Sliding glass doors open the ocean-front façade to a stretch of quiet beach. "The beach is even more beautiful in winter than in summer," says Mr. Wallis. OPPOSITE: Marguerites and ice plant color the peaceful sandscape.

ABOVE: *The Entrance Hall announces the inviting rural atmosphere of the décor. Antique appointments include an 18th-century delft tile stove, a framed crib quilt, a Welsh dresser, and a shepherd's chair near the door.*
OPPOSITE: *A roaring fire warms the raised brick hearth and adds to the cozy cheerfulness of the Living Room. Nearby is a stick-back Windsor chair. The sofa's New Hope quilt-patterned fabric complements a braided rug, one of several found throughout the residence.*

ABOVE: *Broad-arm Windsor chairs and a 17th-century oak table define the Dining Area at one end of the living room. A Dutch brass chandelier, a tall case clock and a gleaming brass container add distinction.*

OPPOSITE ABOVE: *An early Pennsylvania star-patterned quilt is effectively paired with an American pine bench in the second floor Hallway.*

OPPOSITE: *A massive four-poster bed with linenfold headboard paneling dominates the crisp design of Mr. Wallis's Bedroom. An elaborately carved wainscot chair and an oak table used as a desk are both 17th-century.*

FOLLOWING PAGES: *In Mrs. Wallis's Bedroom, a floral print promotes an airy feeling that is furthered by a delicate lace canopy above the 18th-century French field bed. A spindle-back rocker bespeaks unpretentious ease.*

The house in Newport Beach, California, though occupying a splendid setting at the water's edge facing Balboa Island, was simple and unpretentious. There was nothing to suggest that this was the private world of a superstar, an American legend. Nevertheless, before his death in 1980, John Wayne lived here for some fourteen years.

He had long been familiar with Newport Beach, and remembered well the days when it had been no more than a village. "I'm glad I came down here to live fourteen years ago," he said. "I sure as hell couldn't afford it now." The reference to real estate prices in Orange County was appealingly direct. There was, in fact, nothing indirect about John Wayne at all, or about his house. Pretensions had better be left outside.

Nothing, however, is quite that simple, and Mr. Wayne's personality was no exception. He was a man far more complex, far more sophisticated and far more sensitive than his archetypal screen image might have suggested. For example, his house meant a great deal to him—its antiques, its décor, its comforts—and it was hardly a place to throw down the saddlebags and kick a bedroll into the corner.

Mr. Wayne's study, the largest room in the house, presented perhaps the clearest and most compelling image of the man himself. Warm and generous and comfortable, it was most definitely a man's room. The paneling and the fireplace and the small collection of guns strengthened the feeling, and there were many fine examples of western American art—bronzes and prints and oils—as well as a number of American Indian artifacts. A favorite collection of kachina dolls, for example, had been started long ago, in the days when John Wayne used to ride into Monument Valley in Arizona, making films.

Everywhere in the study were the memorabilia of his remarkable career as an actor. The walls around his massive desk contained innumerable photographs and plaques marking the notable events of that career. One wall in particular, rising above a shelf on which rested the Oscar he received for his performance in *True Grit*, was referred to by Mr. Wayne as the "Fifty Years of Hard Work Wall." It was also a record of mem-ories and friendships: pictures of his children; a faded photograph of himself with John Ford, Henry Fonda and Ward Bond, proudly displaying a sailfish they caught near Cabo San Lucas during an outing in the early 1930s.

The memorabilia, the awards, the trophies all attested to the variety of places John Wayne visited, whether making films on location or traveling for pleasure. And for more than thirty years, in the course of these travels, he had been collecting furniture and art and objects of all kinds. The range of his acquisitions was wide and, as he admitted, somewhat haphazard. There were porcelain jardinieres from Honolulu; marvelous figures from Bali, acquired just after World War II; antiques he found in Colorado Springs; furniture from Madrid; figurines from Kyoto; a good deal of impressive Alaskan art.

When making a film on location, nothing gave John Wayne more pleasure than spending his free time browsing through whatever antique shops were available. His curiosity led him everywhere, and he picked up things in many an unlikely place. On the terrace at Newport Beach there was a porcelain table with a pedestal base he found in one of the poorest sections of Puerto Vallarta and, while making a film in Fort Benning, Georgia, he came across an Empire table that became his favorite. His interest in collecting was a compelling one, and it was his habit to take treasured prints or small antiques along with him on location. "You often have to stay for a couple of months in some horrible motel room," he explained. "Well, I like to put a few familiar things on the wall. I try to dress the place up, make it seem more like home."

For home, above all, was what he loved. "Look," he said about Newport Beach, "I find things that appeal to me, and I try to blend them in. I don't give a damn whether anyone else likes them or not." Such words say a great deal about John Wayne. They evoke a particularly human image, in spite of their gruffness—the image of a man of gentleness and sensitivity. And perhaps, in the final analysis, this is a larger and more solid image of John Wayne than the familiar one still to be seen in films.

LEFT: *The Living Room of the late John Wayne's Newport Beach, California home is an expression of the legendary actor's direct personal style. A rugged stone fireplace wall backdrops an eclectic grouping of artworks: A gilt-bronze Thai Buddha is the focal point amid paintings by Nino Caffe, Peter Winter and Russ Vickers. On the low table, enameled bronze figures of a broncobuster and a pony express rider by Harry Jackson make vigorous Western statements.*

ABOVE: *Mirrored walls restate the glitter of a crystal chandelier in the Dining Room. Here, as throughout the residence, are gathered antiques and mementos the actor collected during his worldwide travels.*

LEFT: *Photographs of Mr. Wayne with his family and with film personalities line a Hallway wall. In the image at lower left, actress Fay Wray is mascot for a charity football team of Hollywood's leading men.* **ABOVE**: *The actor called this area of the Study his "Fifty Years of Hard Work Wall." Honors and tributes from all over the world are displayed, highlighted by the 1969 Oscar for Best Actor.*

ABOVE: *Views of Newport Bay contribute to the Master Bedroom's atmosphere of relaxed comfort. An invitingly comfortable conversation grouping provides an ideal vantage point for contemplating the spectacular setting. Sliding glass doors open the room to the vista.*

RIGHT: *Beyond the master bedroom, small benches add a hint of formality to a crisp expanse of brick- and tile-paved Terrace. A swath of lawn and well-tended flowering plants—pansies, marguerites and begonias—salute the nautical panorama. Using an especially appropriate metaphor, John Wayne liked to call his bayside view "not a scene, but a 'moving picture.'"*

CREDITS

JOSEPH ALSOP
photography by Thomas S. Berntsen

FRED ASTAIRE
photography by Russell MacMasters

GEOFFREY BEENE
photography by Jaime Ardiles-Arce
architecture by Philip Haight

CANDICE BERGEN
photography by Jaime Ardiles-Arce
interior design by Renny B. Saltzman

GOV. AND MRS. JOHN Y. BROWN, JR.
photography by Tony Soluri
interior design by R. Wayne Jenkins

JAMES CAAN
photography by Charles S. White
interior design by Robert Cory

ALEXANDER CALDER
photography by Toby Molenaar

GEORGE CUKOR
photography by Russell MacMasters
architecture by James E. Dolena

MR. AND MRS. KIRK DOUGLAS
photography by Russell MacMasters

ERTÉ
photography by Pascal Hinous

MALCOLM FORBES
photography by Pascal Hinous
interior design by Robert Gerofi

HUBERT DE GIVENCHY
photography by Pascal Hinous
interior design by Charles Sévigny

ROBERT GRAVES
photography by Toby Molenaar

GEORGE HAMILTON
photography by Richard Payne
interior design by T. Mikal Scott and
Bill Hamilton

ROY LICHTENSTEIN
photography by Horst

ALI MACGRAW
photography by Russell MacMasters

PRINCESS MARGARET
photography by Derry Moore
architecture by Oliver Messel

ETHEL MERMAN
photography by Jaime Ardiles-Arce
interior design by Carlton Varney

HENRY MOORE
photography by Derry Moore

JEANNE MOREAU
photography by Pascal Hinous

PATRICIA NEAL AND ROALD DAHL
photography by Derry Moore

MIKE NICHOLS
photography by Horst
interior design by Elinor Arnason

CHRISTINA ONASSIS
photography by Pascal Hinous
interior design by Valerian S. Rybar

ZANDRA RHODES
photography by Derry Moore

FRANÇOISE SAGAN
photography by Pascal Hinous

ARNOLD SCAASI
photography by Pascal Hinous

BOBBY SHORT
photography by Elizabeth Heyert

BARBRA STREISAND
photography by Richard Champion

MR. AND MRS. HAL WALLIS
photography by Russell MacMasters
interior design by Harold Levitt, AIA
landscape design by Harvey Wallace Kinnear

JOHN WAYNE
photography by Fritz Taggart

The following writers prepared the original
Architectural Digest articles from which the
material in this book has been adapted:
Charlottte Aillaud, Mario Amaya, Yoric Blumfeld,
Sam Burchell, Peter Carlsen, Roger Cassell, George
Christy, Roald Dahl, Elizabeth Dickson, Christopher
Forbes, Jean-Louis Gaillemin, David Halliday,
Philippe Jullian, Tina Laver, John Loring, Suzanne
Stark Marrow, Toby Molenaar, David Pryce-Jones
All original text adapted by Sam Burchell, Senior
Editor, Architectural Digest.

BOOK DESIGN   Design Office/San Francisco
Peter Martin   Bruce Kortebein   Betsy Perasso

ACKNOWLEDGMENTS

Many staff members and associates of Architectural Digest magazine were instrumental in adapting the original elements and producing the new material which appears in CELEBRITY HOMES II. We appreciate their efforts equally and thank those who were most involved alphabetically:

ALICE BANDY, Vice President, General Manager, The Knapp Press

CECILIA BESSETTE, Executive Assistant, Graphics Coordinator

LYNN BLOCKER, Traffic Coordinator, The Knapp Press

SAM BURCHELL, Senior Editor, Architectural Digest

RICHARD E. BYE, Chairman of the Board, The Knapp Press

GEORGIA GRIGGS, Proofreader

ANTHONY P. IACONO, Production Director, Vice President of Manufacturing, Knapp Communications Corporation

JOANNE JAFFE, Caption Writer

PHILIP KAPLAN, Executive Graphics Director, Knapp Communcations Corporation

BERNICE LIFTON, Copyeditor

JOHN LINCOLN, Antiques Consultant, Architectural Digest

MARGARET REDFIELD, Associate Editor, Architectural Digest

GAYLE MOSS ROSENBERG, Captions Editor, Architectural Digest

CHARLES ROSS, Graphics Director, Architectural Digest

JAN STUEBING, Editorial Assistant, The Knapp Press

DONALD UMNUS, Production Manager, The Knapp Press

ELLEN WINTERS, Production Editor, The Knapp Press

J. KELLY YOUNGER, Managing Editor, Architectural Digest

VERONICA ZAGARINO, Production Coordinator, The Knapp Press